Raising Capital

When You Don't Have a Silicon Valley Address

Interviews with Funding Experts Provide Advice and Insight

Keith Herndon

Foreword by
Ben Dyer

Innovations Publishing
Atlanta, Georgia

RAISING CAPITAL

WHEN YOU DON'T HAVE A SILICON VALLEY ADDRESS

Inquiries to the publisher should be addressed to:

Innovations Publishing, LLC
75 Fifth Street, NW
Suite 311
Atlanta, GA 30308
www.innovationspublising.com

Library of Congress Control Number: 2007937928
International Standard Book Number (ISBN): 978-0-9797729-0-0

Printed in the United States of America

Distributed by:
Itasca Books Distribution
3501 Hwy 100 South
Ste 220
Minneapolis MN 55416
Phone: 952-345-4488
Fax: 952-920-0541
www.itascabooks.com

TABLE OF CONTENTS

Foreword .... Ben Dyer vii

Introduction .... Keith Herndon ix

Chapter 1 .... Knox Massey 1
Atlanta Technology Angels

Chapter 2 .... Sig Mosley 9
Imlay Investments, Inc.

Chapter 3 .... John Mills 19
SBIR Assistance Program, State of Georgia

Chapter 4 .... Lori Whitted 29
Atlanta Life Venture Fund

Chapter 5 .... Wright Steenrod 39
Chrysalis Ventures

Chapter 6 .... Charles Moseley 51
Noro-Moseley Partners

Chapter 7 .... John Huntz 61
Arcapita Ventures

Chapter 8 .... Ted Bender 69
Croft & Bender

Chapter 9 .... Darrell Glasco 79
SVB Silicon Valley Bank

Chapter 10 .... Alan Koenning 89
UPS Strategic Enterprise Fund

Chapter 11 .... Rick Winston 99
E.H. Winston and Associates

Chapter 12 .... Jim Stratigos 111
Jacket Micro Devices

FOREWORD

When Keith Herndon approached us with his idea of creating a book of special interest to entrepreneurs, we immediately suggested he focus on the ever present and ever pressing problem of raising capital. Together we identified twelve individuals representing an array of funding sources and a wide range of viewpoints on this topic. These individuals are daily practitioners in the art of generating capital for newly formed, emerging, or growing companies. We thank all of them for participating in this project, and as you read on you will come to appreciate their genuine expertise in this area.

In regions outside the venture capital centers such as Silicon Valley and Boston, the problem of raising capital is magnified. Investors who have plenty of tempting deals close to home will much prefer those. Most such investors in young companies take board seats, attend monthly meetings, help with business development connections, and provide other services that require physical presence. Why should they fly across the country with all the expense and headaches of air travel as we know it today when they can merely drive across town to generate the same returns?

Of course there are investors who argue strongly that all truly deserving deals do get funded, wherever they may be. They will contend that the really great management teams with bankable ideas are hard to find and are worth searching the country at large. My view is that regions with considerable resident venture capital do give entrepreneurs an edge. They provide frequent networking opportunities that bring together management teams, good ideas, and money. Long ago we funded Peachtree Software with seed capital from Chicago and institutional venture money from Oklahoma and Florida. Atlanta was a real estate town, and even with a strong base of research universities including Georgia Tech, Emory, and Georgia State, the money that had been made here had been made in something other than technology and was looking for more of the same opportunities that had worked well before. I gave serious thought to moving to San Jose; almost for no other reason than to be part of the regular Friday poker games that many of my peer pioneers in microcomputer software applications were attending. The deals were getting done there, the capital was being formed, and the trends were being identified. I was 2,110 miles removed from the action. Nonetheless we stayed in place and enjoyed a very successful outcome at Peachtree Software, and there have since been many more and many much larger wins in Atlanta. The intent of this book is not to debate the esoteric issues but to provide some practical advice that those seeking capital can put to good use.

I would like to thank Keith Herndon for his excellent work in conducting and editing this collection of interviews, and I would also like to recognize my colleague Buddy Ray (coincidentally the first programmer hired by Peachtree Software) for his considerable efforts in bringing together all the elements of this project. We hope you enjoy this book and will always welcome your comments, suggestions or criticisms on this topic. If you like what you read, let us know, and we may just tackle some other topics of value to entrepreneurs.

-Ben Dyer, President, Innovations Publishing

INTRODUCTION

An entrepreneur is someone who dares to dream the dreams and is foolish enough to try to make those dreams come true.[1]

Vinod Khosla, Legendary Venture Capitalist

The following collection of interviews was compiled for the purpose of providing entrepreneurs with a deeper insight into the process of raising capital. The interviews are intended to take entrepreneurs inside the process; to show how leading experts in the field think about what they do and to give them a forum for sharing that insight with entrepreneurs.

The timing of our interview project coincides with a surge in capital raising activity. Traditional venture capital investments are at their highest levels since 2001,[2] and there has been a significant increase in corporate venture capital activity as well.[3] The MoneyTree Report by PricewaterhouseCoopers and the National Venture Capital Association (NVCA), using data from Thomson Financial, showed that traditional venture capital funds invested $7.1 billion in 977 deals during the second quarter of 2007. This was the largest quarterly investment by venture capital funds since the end of 2001. During that same second quarter, corporate venture funds invested another $1.3 billion in 390 deals, also the largest inflow of corporate dollars into the venture market since 2001.[4]

"Venture capitalists have found no shortage of promising companies in which to invest . . . . Innovation is alive and well," commented Tracy Lefteroff, global managing partner of the venture capital practice at PricewaterhouseCoopers.[5] In speaking about the level of corporate venture, Mark Heesen, president of the NVCA, said that "despite uncertainty in the

U.S. economy" companies were investing at the "highest levels post-bubble," adding that if the pace continued, "we could see all-time record levels [in corporate venture]."[6]

This surge in venture activity remains far below the peak of the dot com explosion when $28.4 billion was invested in the first quarter of 2000, but it represents a remarkable comeback since the low point of 2003.[7] The recent upswing may be tempting many entrepreneurs to strike out with new ventures, sensing that funding will be easier to obtain.

The reality, however, is that it remains a buyer's market. Those with capital to invest can pick and choose from the best companies. The trend is that more venture capital investment is gravitating toward later stage companies and less money is going into start-up businesses. Of the second quarter totals referenced earlier, 44 percent of that $7.1 billion went to later stage companies, while only 3.1 percent went to start-up companies.[8] Andrew Metrick, an associate professor of finance at the Wharton School of the University of Pennsylvania, said that venture capitalists fund less than 1 percent of all start-ups, forcing the other 99 percent to look for alternative funding through angel investors or other sources of money such as debt financing.[9] In understanding that reality, we have included among our interview subjects those experts with backgrounds in angel investing, government grants, debt financing and alternative financing.

Also, as the title of our compilation suggests, geography was a theme that we explored throughout the interviews. The data clearly indicates that more venture capital is invested in Silicon Valley than in anywhere else in the country. In the second quarter data, for example, $2.5 billion, or 35.5 percent of the total, went to companies based in Silicon Valley, while only $356 million, or 5 percent of the total, went to companies based in the Southeast. Therefore, companies without a Silicon Valley address must work very hard to get noticed, and in many cases that will involve a national search for money. For example, the Southeast Venture Conference, citing data from Thompson Financial, said that 81 percent of the venture investment in the Southeast originates from outside the region. [10]

At the height of the venture capital boom in 1999, Harvard researchers Paul Gompers and Josh Lerner published "The Venture Capital Cycle," a book that took a serious academic look at the venture capital industry, its history and its cyclical nature. They attempted to answer questions regarding the sustainability of the industry, and in the end the researchers concluded that "the increasing familiarity with the venture capital process has itself made the long-term prospects for venture investment more attractive than they have ever been before. . ."[11] The events of the past decade have borne out their conclusion; the venture capital industry rode out the post-bubble storm and emerged once again as a familiar, vital part of the financial industry landscape.

As you read the following dozen interviews, you will also become more familiar with the capital raising process and will come to appreciate that is more art than science. Entrepreneurs who master the process will understand that networking and building solid management teams are the factors that count most, whether you have a Silicon Valley address or not.

- Keith Herndon

---

[1] http://www.khoslaventures.com/

[2] MoneyTree Report by PricewatershouseCoopers at https://www.pwcmoneytree.com.

[3] Ibid.

[4] Ibid.

[5] National Venture Capital Association and PricewaterhouseCoopers Press Release, August 7, 2007.

[6] National Venture Capital Association and PricewaterhouseCoopers Press Release, August 30, 2007.

[7] MoneyTree Report by PricewatershouseCoopers at https://www.pwcmoneytree.com.
[8] Ibid.
[9] "Capturing Value from Entrepreneurial Start-ups," Wall Street Journal Blogs at http://blogs.wsj.com/ups/2007/06/01/capturing-value-from-entrepreurrial-start-up/.
[10] http://seventure.org/SoutheastVentureConference/40/southeast-venture-returns-investment.
[11] "The Venture Capital Cycle," Paul Gompers and Josh Lerner, MIT Press, 1999.

CHAPTER 1

Knox Massey, Managing Director
Atlanta Technology Angels

In his role of Managing Director at ATA, Massey has helped raise funding for Invistics, Qcept Technologies, Fortel DTV, Oversight Systems, OpenSpan Software, Jacket Micro Devices, Asankya, Zeewise, Beacon Software, Invirtus, Pranama and Aretta. Massey has also participated in the execution of an additional 30+ financing rounds associated with ATA portfolio companies, six M&A events and two shutdowns. Massey is currently an investor in ATA portfolio companies Marketworks, Market Velocity and Beacon Software. Prior to his role at ATA, Massey held senior sales positions at America Online, served in a management position at the WestWayne Advertising Agency and worked within regional sales offices of the New York Times Regional Newspaper Group. He sits on the Board of Directors of ATA and the Angel Capital Association. He also serves as a general partner of Keith-Massey Partnership, LLLP. Massey holds an MBA from the GEM Program at Georgia State University and holds Series 7 and Series 63 securities licenses.

Q: Angel investors are mentioned often as a source of funding for emerging growth companies. Can you set the foundation for this discussion by defining what the term "angel investor" means?

A: An angel investor is someone using personal money versus what we call "other people's money" (OPM). So, when you make an angel investment, you reach around to your back pocket and pull out your checkbook and write a check. It's not a pooled source of capital or pooled capital that is raised from pension funds, endowments or from corporations. It's usually from individuals who made their money through investments or had a nice exit of their own from an entrepreneurial venture. So it's very local and very personal money.

Q: How would you describe the climate for angel investing as we near the end of this decade?

A: It's a lot better than in 2002 when I first started as Managing Director at ATA! Industries go in cycles, and the angel investing industry – to categorize it one way – is seeing a nice "uptick." The economy is certainly stronger than in 2002, and in 2007 we're seeing a lot of private equity type deals, and nice positive exits from earlier investments that were made in 1999-2002. We also see a lot more interest in angel investing in Atlanta – and across the nation for that matter – because the angels have gotten much more professional, more experienced, and there is much more process to this type of investing.

Q: What has been some of the biggest changes you have seen in angel investing since you became involved with it?

A: I became involved with the Atlanta Technology Angels in 2001, but did individual investing in 1999 and 2000. (ATA was formed in 1998.) I started as Managing Director of ATA in 2002. At that time I was frustrated trying to figure out how to deal with some angel investing issues we had locally. I began to notice that groups like ours across the country were beginning to form and they all wanted to operate more professionally. I started reaching out, and over time found a number of other groups to talk to in North Carolina and Florida. By 2004, the Angel Capital Association had formed, which now links together 125 groups from across the nation. So, now in 2007, I have a forum to talk to these groups on a regular basis; groups in North Carolina and California and Boston and Tennessee and so on. So, the biggest change I've seen is the growth of these angel groups and the connections they provide regionally and nationally.

Q: What has been the impetus behind the formation of these groups; is it to facilitate deal flow?

A: It's really a cost and time efficiency analysis. Individual angels were finding that it took them a lot of time and effort and money to look at multiple angel investment opportunities. And in the case of certain technologies – say a healthcare opportunity came their way – they had to spend a lot of time and effort on due diligence because their expertise might not be in healthcare. As a result, individual investors were slow to invest. The more formalized angel groups brought the individual angels together and started building processes. These groups then had an ability to look at deals on a faster basis, a more efficient basis and more competent basis. Also, you could pool the "personal" capital together to make bigger chunks of an investment that would help the company. It has been good for the companies as well because it often took a lot of time and effort on both sides to get an investment done. It's much easier to get an investment made when angels are all together.

Q: With the advent of these angel groups, do you find that most angel investors work as part of a group or are there still a significant number of angels investing independently?

A: I would say it is more common to find the groups. It has also moved beyond just getting together to see deals. A lot of people have been involved for years and have become friends and have invested in a number of companies together. There is a social aspect to it. You still find individual angels out there, but in the larger markets like Boston and Texas and California and New York and Atlanta, you will find that the entrepreneurs talk amongst themselves and find it more efficient to approach the angel groups.

Q: Your group is based in Atlanta; do you find the Southeast as being a particularly active region for angel investment?

A: One of the earliest angel groups that I am aware of is an angel group in North Carolina called TIG, which stands for Tri-State Investment Group. It was founded in 1989, I believe. and TIG is really the granddaddy of angel groups in the Southeast, and also in the nation. I think they have four or five angel funds. North Carolina has a great state tax incentive that encourages the formation of "angel" funds. You will find a number of other groups in North Carolina. Greensboro, Winston-Salem and Raleigh have become a hot bed of angel groups because of the tax incentives that the state has. You will also find groups in South Carolina – Charleston – and you will find a number of groups in Florida. In Georgia, outside of Atlanta, there are groups in Savannah and Augusta. Other groups are in Kentucky and Tennessee – so yes, it's very active here.

Q: Are the types of deals angel investors see today different from those say a decade ago?

A: Concepts on napkins getting angel funding are a thing of the past.

Q: What are the industry segments that stand out as being especially attractive to angel investors?

A: You have to look at the market and see what the market is offering. And that changes about every year or two. Right now healthcare is pretty active and biotech is pretty active in the angel community–although ATA rarely funds either. We obviously feel that technology is a good investment in Atlanta and we do a lot of funding through Georgia Tech. There is a lot of opportunity with the Emory University community as well.

Q: Looking at it from the entrepreneur's perspective, what have you found to be the best method of approach for entrepreneurs seeking to attract an angel investment?

A: Companies should come to us earlier rather than later. I think a lot of companies and entrepreneurs have been erroneously guided to get their company to a certain level and then wrap a nice red ribbon on the company and shotgun it out to the investor community. I find that doesn't work that well. I always tell young companies to get to us early. It may not be the time for an investment, but we get to know more about the principals and learn more about the company. When it is the right time to raise capital, it is an easier discussion.

Q: Is there a rule of thumb you would suggest to an entrepreneur for knowing when the time is right to graduate from self-funding or friends and family money and begin seeking outside investment?

A: There is no hard set time frame for raising an investment. I suggest to the entrepreneur to get to know the people that are investing in these companies because the investors may know when the time is right for an investment. Perhaps a good time to raise capital is when an entrepreneur has capital requirements that he can't meet from friends and family. Perhaps when the company needs to be accelerated; maybe they're early to a particular market but they are starting to see some competition and they need to grow more quickly to capture more of the market, etc.

Q: At these early stages of funding, how do angel investors typically approach the question of valuation?

A: You'll find most angel groups now are pretty comfortable with valuation. ATA has been around for eight years. A lot of these other angel groups have been around for five, six, seven or eight years and they've done a lot of deals. They understand the metrics and the terms of a typical deal and are comfortable with the valuation. Remember, it's a two way street between an entrepreneur and the early stage investors. It should be a conversation that is really about how we are going to work together and how are we both going to make money together. It's not how can I take advantage of you or how you get the advantage of me. That's not what it's about; it's about building companies and encouraging entrepreneurs and hopefully in the end everybody makes money and everybody's happy.

Q: How much equity would an angel investor typically seek in exchange for early funding?

A: It's variable. An angel or entrepreneur would have to look at that geographically as well. I'd say anywhere from 5 percent to 50 percent. If the company is going to be a lifestyle company and an angel is putting in $1 milllion, maybe 50 percent is correct. If the company is going to need $20 million pre-exit, that's a different conversation and it's a different valuation. There is no hard and fast rule. The most important thing to do is to try and look two to three years down the line to envision where the company wants to be and then work backwards to get the equity stake and capital needed.

Q: When approaching an angel group, how important is it to have a prepared business plan?

A: A business plan is good to have, but you don't need a 75-page business plan to impress the investor. A basic business plan is good to have because it really makes the entrepreneur think through how they will build the company. It is not absolutely necessary for an investment however. I generally prefer a 2- to 5-page executive summary.

Q: So what elements would you expect to see in a business plan for an early stage company?

A: Let's refer to the executive summary I mentioned in the last question. The entrepreneur needs to very quickly describe what the company does and describe the products and/or service. You need to talk about the competition. Don't tell us there is no competition, because there is an almost guarantee there is. You need to tell the investor why the company and management team are unique. You need to tell the investors why they should back the management team as well as the product and service. You should tell the investor how the money is going to be spent and how you are going to sell the company. The investor is putting in the money expecting to get a monetary return at some future point, so the scenario of how that happens should be explained.

Q: How much effort should an entrepreneur put into creating financial projections? Do angel investors put much credence in these projections?

A: We want to see that the company has put some effort into it. But, be realistic. A business plan forces you to say how you are structuring the company, and it shows you've gone through effort and that you have put a lot of time and passion into thinking how the company is going to be built and run, so it's good to see that. But are we wedded to the financial projections, and do we always believe them? Probably not. If you project you're going to do $4 million next year and you do $1 million, you've got a long board meeting saying why you missed the numbers.

Q: What do you see as the biggest mistake entrepreneurs make when approaching a potential angel investor?

A: I am always surprised that the entrepreneurs don't conduct due diligence on the investors. Most entrepreneurs take a shot gun approach and don't consider the strategies of the investors – funds or angels. I always suggest you understand as much as you can about the investor or group that you are talking to. If the investor group knows that you understand what they are trying to do, it's going to be a much easier conversation.

Q: Do you have any other advice that would make the process of raising capital go more smoothly?

A: I want to reiterate what I just mentioned: Try to understand whom you are talking to. And as we talked about earlier, make sure that you've done a competent executive summary or short business plan. And don't expect a check to come out of the first meeting. You are trying to get to that second meeting. Once you come in and talk to our group, you want to get enough interest that 15 angels want to go to the next meeting and do detailed due diligence.

CHAPTER 2

Sig Mosley
President
Imlay Investments, Inc.

Mosley is President of Imlay Investments, Inc., the personal investment company of John P. Imlay, Jr. He joined Management Science America, Inc. (merged into Dun & Bradstreet Software Services, Inc.) in 1969 as a staff accountant, served as Secretary-Treasurer from 1972 to 1990 and was a Vice President from 1982 to 1991. Mosley received his Bachelor of Business Administration from Emory University in 1968. From 1968 to 1969, he was employed by Peat Marwick & Mitchell as a staff accountant. Mosley serves on the board of directors of the following private companies: Bancintelligence; Contract Packaging, Inc., eQuorum Corporation; Rotunda Corporation; Invistics, Inc.; Kelly Registration, Inc.; Photobooks, Inc.; Pramana; SciHealth, Inc.; Skyway Software, Inc.; and USBA Holdings, Inc. In addition, Mosley is a Director of The Imlay Foundation, Inc., Techbridge, Technology Association of Georgia, and Entrepreneurs Foundation of the Southeast. Mosley is also a director of GATV.

Q: How did Imlay Investments get started?

A: We began in 1990 after John Imlay sold Management Science America (MSA) to Dun and Bradstreet. We wanted to give back to the community in two ways. First, we created a charitable foundation called The Imlay Foundation to give to charities in the Atlanta area, and, seond, we wanted to give entrepreneurs the opportunity to grow a business like we were able to grow MSA. MSA began with five Georgia Tech grads, and over the years the Atlanta community was very good to MSA, so John and I wanted to give back. We began doing angel investing in 1990 before it was actually called angel investing.

Q: What is the investment philosophy behind your firm?

A: We've been at this for over 18 years and we have done about 88 deals; we have 28 deals that we are still in. We do primarily early stage deals, the very early funding: seed rounds to the A rounds. We are primarily into technology: IT, software, infrastructure, Internet and a chip deal every now and then. We try to invest in what we understand, and part of what we try to do is give the entrepreneur an opportunity to work with us and to help educate him on how to grow the business.

Q: Would Imlay Investments be considered an angel investor, or are you beyond that in terms of investment stage?

A: I think the current term for what we do is super angel. The traditional angel is generally investing from $25,000 to $100,000. The super angel will tend to invest larger amounts, but not as large as the VCs (venture capitalists) would invest. Our initial investment is anywhere from $100,000 to $300,000 and we'll go up to about $1 million over the life of a single company. We will come in between the friends and family, angel round and the initial institutional round. Sometimes we will come in as a part of the institutional round as well.

Q: With that perspective, would you give us your impression of the capital raising market for these early stage companies?

A: For an early stage company, particularly in the Southeast, it is very difficult to raise money. The number of angels that we have in the community has shrunk due to the dot com bust and the telecom bust. A number of early stage VC firms that were in Atlanta have gone away, and the remaining VC funds tend to invest at a later stage rather than the very early stage. Here you only have the Atlanta Technology Angels group that we are involved with and a few independent angels that are still active. Now when you get outside of the Southeast, angel and start-up capital is much more plentiful in areas such as Silicon Valley and Boston. For later stage companies, especially those with revenue and a track record, capital is much more readily available.

Q: What are the factors that you think have led to the Southeast being under served in the capital raising process? Are there structural factors in play?

A: One of the structural things is that I think the motivation of the entrepreneurs to be repeat entrepreneurs is lacking. We don't have as many repeat entrepreneurs as other regions and part of that is based upon cultural differences here in the Southeast. An entrepreneur makes $10 million here; he'll go buy a beach house and a boat and will be happy not to do it again. Where in other regions, I think there may be more entrepreneurial drive to do it over and over again. Now that's not to say that we don't have repeat entrepreneurs because we have some good ones. It's just that we don't have the volume of repeat entrepreneurs that I think other regions have.

Q: Is this due to a regional bias of sort? Does the region make it harder for entrepreneurs to go out and take a risk because if it doesn't work they might be branded as a failure more so than they would in another region?

A: I don't know that I would agree with that. Personally, I have a case where we had an entrepreneur and the company just did not make it, but it was market timing and not related to anything that he did wrong. We backed him in a second opportunity. There is a chance you could get branded to a degree, but I think that if there are valid reasons why the company didn't make it, then the entrepreneur can overcome that.

Q: If you were an entrepreneur with a good idea, would it make sense to relocate to the Silicon Valley, or could you be just as successful in the Southeast?

A: It all depends on what industry and what market segments you are going after. There are definitely certain market segments where the West Coast has more opportunity for getting money and customers. You would also have look at where the management talent is. Trying to build a semi-conductor company, for example in Atlanta – the Southeast – would be very difficult because we just don't have the management talent in the semi conductor area. You have to look at where your talent is.

Q: Have you found certain industries or segments that are especially attractive for early stage capital given the market conditions as we near the end of the decade?

A: Security software is one that is attracting a lot of investment. Two of our last four investments have been in the security software area. The wireless area still has a lot of attraction. A couple of areas that we don't invest in with our funds, but are still very hot from a market perspective are biotechnology and nanotechnology. We do not invest in those segments because I do not have knowledge in that area. There is a lot of money going into social networking technology, but I think you will find soon that there is going to have to be some consolidation in that area.

Q: When you find an opportunity you like, do you invest alone or typically with other co-investors?

A: Our initial investments are generally done where we will bring in co-investors. I almost never invest by myself anymore. We have done that, but it proved to be more work than we really wanted. There are times that a VC is looking at a very early stage deal, but they don't happen to be local. They may want a local investor and will approach us about joining the deal to be their eyes and ears here. We also co-invest with the ATA (Atlanta Technology Angels). We co-invest with independent angels and we have actually done co-investment deals with VC firms here when the deal is early stage. We also have a good working relationship with a number of Boston, Mid-Atlantic and West Coast firms.

Q: Are you seeing more of a willingness for these funds in Boston and Silicon Valley to come into the Southeast more so now than they were doing a few years ago?

A: Oh, yes. I don't think there is any question about that. Now, they are doing deals at a little later stage and not at the real early stage, but there are exceptions. Sigma Partners out of Boston is in three of my deals right now. Matrix has come in recently, and Battery Ventures is active here. There are a number of firms coming into town and finding good deals.

Q: As an early stage investor, you must have a long investment horizon. How long do you expect to be in a deal before there is an exit?

A: For the early stage deal today you go into it anticipating that you will be in the deal 5 to 7 years. It just takes longer today to build a company up and to create the value required. As for the exit strategy – it's been very interesting that over the 17 years I've been doing this, I've had only two companies to go public – Internet Security Systems and Witness Systems. The vast majority of our exits have been through M&A activity, and I think you will see that continuing especially in the Southeast. We tend to build companies that get bought by other companies; we don't tend to take many companies public here.

Q: Are the entrepreneurs on board with these expectations? A 5- to 7-year horizon for an exit event means that the entrepreneur must have a passion for the idea and you have to be comfortable they have the patience and persistence to

see it through. Are you seeing entrepreneurs with that understanding of the market?

A: I think that with the first-time entrepreneur there is an education process. They always come in with an attitude that it is going to happen quicker and easier than it really does. Once they get into it, they begin to realize the difficulties they may run into, and so for the most part, I think they are willing to accept that kind of time horizon. Seasoned entrepreneurs recognize what they are up against when they are doing their second or third or fourth one; they realize what the potential time period can be and are more accepting of it.

Q: Overall, how has the nature of entrepreneurship changed over the years that you've been doing this?

A: We went through a period in the early 90s when most of our deals were with the first time entrepreneur. They came in with an optimistic attitude, but they also came with the attitude that they wanted to build a company. They really wanted to build a big company and one that would have lasting, long-term value. By the late 90s with the Internet boom, the attitude changed and everybody wanted to build a company and sell it immediately. That was fine as long as money was plentiful and valuations kept going up. But after we went through the dot com bust and people were finding it hard to get money, there was a trend to "we don't necessarily need to be entrepreneurs; we'll just go to work for the P&Gs or the J&Js." That was especially true of those coming out of grad school. I think currently entrepreneurs are still a little shell shocked because it is hard to raise money. Therefore, I think you will find that the entrepreneur of today is probably more like the entrepreneurs in the early 90s. They are striving to build a company and are not motivated by the bubble mentality.

Q: In evaluating a prospective investment, do you put more emphasis on the entrepreneur or the idea the entrepreneur is bringing to you?

A: That's an interesting question. You have to look at the entrepreneur. At MSA, we had a motto "People are the Key" and that has always been something that we believe in. If you read John Imlay's book, he talks about being a tiger in business. So you've got to have the right people in the company. In addition to the right people, you've got to have a market. As I have told many people, you can have the best people and the best product, but if you don't have a market that wants to buy your product, you are not going to make it. So I think it is a combination of people and markets, and you have to look at both of them.

Q: Specific to the entrepreneur, what qualities do you look for in an individual and how do you evaluate if a person you are talking with has what you are seeking?

A: We look for a core set of values: honesty and trust and passion for the idea. You've got to have an entrepreneur that's got passion about what he's doing. But you also have to have more than passion. You also have to have somebody who has good ideas about how to approach the business. We want somebody who will listen to advice when something may not be going right. You have to evaluate the entrepreneur based on his ability to react to situations. You have to look at the quality of people he surrounds himself with. You may have someone that looks like he could be a great entrepreneur, but if the people he selects to be his cohorts are not of the same caliber then that says something about his ability to build a team. It's really more of a gut feeling after having spent time with the person. But you can't always know how it will turn out. We had one entrepreneur who was very good during the good times, but when the situation turned and it came time to lay off people and cut salaries, he couldn't do it. He didn't perform well in the crisis, and you don't necessarily know that up front.

Q: From the time you find a potential opportunity to the time you make an investment, what is the period of courtship? How long does it typically take for you to make an investment decision?

A: It can be anywhere from four weeks to six months. Part of it depends upon what I know about the marketplace already. Part of it depends on whether or not we are dealing with a seasoned entrepreneur. Somebody I have previously invested in makes it a very easy decision process. But when we have to get to know the person, it takes a little bit longer.

Q: How much emphasis do you put on a business plan when evaluating these early stage companies?

A: You need to see that the entrepreneur knows his market and that he knows his business model and that he knows who his competitors are. So you need a document that can lead the business plan – maybe it would be better called a marketing plan. You want to be sure that the entrepreneur has done his homework. I have told a lot of entrepreneurs, that if you come to me and tell me you have no competitors, I'll tell you that you haven't done your market research. You don't know your market yet if you think there isn't any competition. And I'm not only interested in who the competitors are today, but who the competitors could be tomorrow. So you really need to be able to write a plan that outlines your business model. The numbers are the last thing I ever look at in a plan, because I don't believe any numbers. I can make up any set of numbers you want. What the numbers should be is a realistic reflection of the opportunity. The plan has to be about convincing me that the entrepreneur knows the market. And if he can't convey that in a written document, then you worry about the entrepreneur's ability to communicate.

Q: If you were an entrepreneur yourself – not someone giving out the money – what's the one thing you would do to set yourself up to get funding?

A: Unfortunately, I'm not sure you can do one thing. It's many things. The first thing you've got to do is research and understand your market. You need to go out and make sure you know what the market is you are going after, and that includes competitors. Then you need to try to make sure you understand what your business model is, and then you need to get good advisors around you. It is very important when you go out to raise money, that you can show your ability to attract respected people from your industry onto an advisory board. That lends a lot of credibility.

Q: How important is it at the early stage to have a working prototype of the product?

A: In these early stage deals, it is not necessary. We're not expecting the level of funding to have been there to build a prototype; in some cases we've made deals where we didn't even have a completed business model, but we knew what the market was. Now, you do need a good technologist who can help convince me that you know how to get there with the technology that you have.

Q: How should an entrepreneur with an idea approach you about funding?

A: Well, cold calling is not the way to do it. You need to find somebody who can make an introduction for you. Because if somebody I know and trust introduces you to me, I will spend more time looking at your plan than I would if I get a call or email from you and I have no idea who you are. I think that is a part of your advisors' role; get advisors who help make introductions. Also, entrepreneurs must take the time to know who they are dealing with; to learn who we are. There have been at least 20 people sit in our conference room and confidently tell me they understand our investment philosophy because they have researched us and read our website. That is a dead giveaway that they haven't a clue because we don't have a website. You should hear the backpedaling when we point that out.

CHAPTER 3

John Mills, Director
SBIR Assistance Program
State of Georgia

As Director of the SBIR Assistance Program for the State of Georgia, Mills is charged with promoting the Small Business Innovation Research program to Georgia companies, helping them understand the program and assisting with submitting quality proposals. In the previous four years as Manager of Technical Marketing for Georgia Tech's NASA Southeast Regional Technology Transfer Center, Mills worked with over 100 companies in supplying information and reviewing proposals. He has given workshops on the program from Cleveland to Miami. He has worked in technology transfer at Georgia Tech for over twenty years with prior engineering and management experience in industry. Mills received a Bachelor's degree in Industrial Engineering from Georgia Tech in 1971, an MBA from Armstrong Atlantic State University in 1979 and is a graduate of the Engineer Officer Advanced Course. He is a Registered Professional Engineer, a Senior Member in the Institute of Industrial Engineers, and has held various offices in the Georgia Society of Professional Engineers, including State President.

Q: When entrepreneurs begin thinking about the process of raising capital, the first sources they usually consider are friends and family, angel investors and venture firms that specialize in early stage companies. But there are other interesting funding alternatives. One of these is the Small Business Innovation Research Program, or SBIR. Would you give us an overview of the program and a little of its history?

A: The program was started almost 25 years ago when there was a realization that the federal government wasn't really able to easily tap into some of the new ideas being developed by small companies and small companies were having a hard time breaking into the federal research and development game. This program was established as a set aside of 2.5 percent of the external research budget of federal agencies that have at least $100 million in research funded outside their agency. The purpose is so the federal agencies can tap into new ideas that would help them with their mission and that these companies can participate with the federal government without having to compete against major defense contractors. At least once a year each of the 11 participating federal agencies will publish a list of topics that they're interested in. The listings will have deadlines for receiving proposals for funding.

Q: Are there established guidelines that establish how much a grant under this program is worth to the recipient?

A: The initial phase, or Phase I, is typically six months of funding at $100,000. This allows the company to do a feasibility study to show that their technology is workable and will address all the problems the federal agency wants to resolve. If that is successful the company may submit a Phase II funding request for up to two years of funding at typically a $750,000 level. In this phase, the company is expected to produce and test a prototype. It is intended at that point if they have something that's worthwhile that they will be able to attract additional funding from outside the SBIR to finish the commercialization of the product and to get it to market.

Q: How does the SBIR program compare to the Small Business Technology Transfer program known as the STTR? Are these programs complementary?

A: Yes. The Small Business Technology Transfer program, or STTR as it is known, was established several years after SBIR. It was realized that the SBIR program really wasn't tapping some of the new ideas coming out of universities as well as it should. So, it is a requirement of STTR that a company partner with a non-profit research institute, which typically means a research university, to submit a proposal. The company and the university each must contribute significantly to the research and development of the project. Beyond that it's very similar to the SBIR.

Q: How much money has the government set aside to fund the SBIR and the STTR programs?

A: As I mentioned, the SBIR is 2.5 percent of the federal government's external research budget for the participating agencies and the STTR is 0.3 percent. Over the years the total amount committed to the program has been growing. For the current year it is $2.2 billion.

Q: That's quite a large set aside. Is all of that money used each year?

A: Yes. As mandated by law every cent of it is used.

Q: Would you describe the basic qualifications a business must demonstrate in order to be eligible for these programs?

A: Well, the basic qualification is that it has to be a small business. And by that definition it has to have fewer than 500 employees. In actuality, 75 percent of the companies that are participating and winning awards are under 25 employees, and many of those have less than a handful of employees. So it really is aimed at small business. The company also has to be owned primarily by U.S. citizens or legal residents. The work has to be done almost exclusively in the United States unless there is some compelling reason that part of it has to be done outside the United States.

Q: If a company receives an SBIR grant, are there strings attached to this? By that I mean is this an outright grant? If the government isn't taking an equity position what are the obligations on the part of the recipient company?

A: A company that receives an SBIR award loses no equity and does not have to pay money back. Essentially, the obligation is to do the research and development that the company says they were going to do and to issue reports at the end of the period of performance. If they find the work doesn't do what they thought it would do, then they are really under no further obligation but to say we tried to do this and it didn't work. On the other hand, if it did work, here are the results and here is our proposal for Phase II so we can carry on that work. The one caveat is that the federal government retains a royalty free license on any intellectual property coming out of the work. That starts to worry some entrepreneurs, but in a practical sense, the government is just interested in getting that product to market. If the company that has developed the intellectual property decides not to pursue getting that product to market, then the government retains the right to have somebody else pursue it. The government almost never exercises that right because if the product is of value to the government, it is worthwhile for the company to complete the development and sell the product back to the government.

Q: Would the government's retention of the royalty free license obligate the recipient company to pay any royalty fees to the agency in the future if a product is successful? Are there any types of future revenue share arrangements?

A: No. It's strictly the company's property and they can do with it what they wish without royalties or any other obligations to the government.

Q: Can you describe the application process so that the entrepreneurs reading this can get a sense of the level of effort involved in receiving a grant of this type?

A: Yes, it is free government money, so there are quite a few people who would like to obtain these grants. The application process is thorough and competitive. Approximately one out of seven Phase I proposals gets funded. When you get beyond that to the Phase II level, usually 40-50 percent of those get funded but you have to go through Phase I first. It takes – particularly for a first time proposal – upwards of 100 man-hours of effort to put together a decent proposal.

Q: How long does the process take before a company would know if they actually receive a grant? Please describe more about the entire process.

A: Once you submit your proposal, it will take from four to nine months for the agency to evaluate the proposal depending on the agency. Some of the smaller agencies actually have taken longer. Then even after selecting the winning proposals, it takes another month or two to get the grant in place.

Q: Is the time frame similar for Phase II funding?

A: After the six months performance period for Phase I, there is an evaluation period of several months for the Phase II proposal. If approved, there will be another month or two to get that grant in place. Then you would begin the two year period of performance for Phase II. So overall, we're looking at about a four year process from the time you say I'm interested in submitting an SBIR proposal to the time you finish your Phase II work. This timing obviously does not work with all companies, but when it does, it is some really good money.

Q: You mentioned earlier that these monies are coming from a budget set aside from various agencies, but it is my understanding that the Small Business Administration coordinates the program. How does the relationship work between the SBA and the various agencies?

A: The SBA has overall administrative oversight. They try to see that everyone is following the overall rules. But each of the 11 different agencies put their own twists to the program. So there really isn't just one SBIR program; there are really 11 different SBIR programs, and even within the Department of Defense, there are a number of different variations. The SBIR has been in existence for almost 25 years and over the years it has evolved in each government agency so that there are significant differences in the level of funding, the way the proposals are put together, and how it is administered. So, everyone that gets involved in the program has to look at the particular agency and how that agency goes about the program.

Q: You had mentioned at the beginning of this interview about the award levels, but could you give more specifics about what a company should expect to receive in Phase I and Phase II?

A: The typical limits of Phase I is $100,000 for six months. Now there are some agencies that have lower limits as they try to stretch the dollars out. On the other hand, there are a few agencies that will let you exceed that limit if you can justify it. For example, the National Institutes of Health very often will allow significant increases over that $100,000 level. Similarly in Phase II, the typical level is $750,000; some agencies are less. For instance, the Department of Agriculture Phase II is only $350,000. Again, the National Institutes of Health regularly exceeds the $750,000 level. Also, we have one company we've been working with recently that received a $1.8 million Phase II grant from the Department of Defense. This was somewhat unusual, but that does happen.

Q: With this level of funding available, what types of companies are best-suited for applying for these grants?

A: We work with a really wide range of types of companies. Some are well established companies; some are just very basic, one-person start ups working out of their garage. Probably the most typical is a very early stage company that has some good science and is looking for very early stage seed capital. We also work with companies that have developed the technology to a greater extent and are looking to explore a secondary market or a secondary application for their basic science. And occasionally, we are working with established manufacturers that have an R&D effort that are looking to expand in new areas. Probably the common thread is that the companies have to have some recognizable talent in research and development.

Q: Are there examples of a few companies that successfully used the SBIR program that you are familiar with?

A: One that really jumps to mind is Radatec, which was a Georgia Tech VentureLab company that also came up through the Advanced Technology Development Center here at Georgia Tech. They were two guys that were employees of the Georgia Tech Research Institute and were working on radar technology. They saw an application for the work they were doing to monitor high speed turbines and they received permission to explore commercializing that technology outside of Georgia Tech. They applied for and received a NASA Phase I and a NASA Phase II as well as a National Science Foundation Phase I and Phase II over a period of about five years. This SBR funding provided most of the money that they needed over this period, and it allowed them to perfect their technology, which was eventually purchased by a large international controls company. The principals are now working for that large company and have done quite well through the acquisition of their company.

Q: That's an excellent example of a success story. Are there typical mistakes companies make when applying for these programs that could be avoided?

A: Yes, there are a variety of ways to go wrong. One common error is not doing the homework. A lot of companies and individuals who are starting up companies think they have a good idea but they're not really up on what's going on in the rest of the world in that area of technology. They start to write a proposal and are not able to distinguish what they are doing from what the rest of the state-of-the-art is doing. So they really can't sell the uniqueness of their technology and that becomes a drawback. Another mistake is not adequately addressing the commercialization of the proposed technology development. SBIR funding is different from many other government research grants in that it is supposed to lead to an actual product that is put to use. Some early stage companies have a good handle on the technology and how to develop it, but they lack experience in how a product will be manufactured and finally reach the marketplace. The science must be there, but increasingly the government is also looking at whether a company understands who is going to buy their technology and how the company is going to serve that market.

Q: Have you found that companies who successfully win one of these grants have an easier time raising other forms of capital? Does the process of creating the business plan and completing the grant process instill a discipline that translates into other capital raising activities?

A: Oh certainly. You know an example that comes to mind is a company that's working in the Ethanol area. We worked with them a couple of years ago when they were just starting to get off the ground with a proposal, and it wasn't funded. But the exercise they went through was really the first time that they had done anything like that, and it gave them the experience to go forward and prepare other proposals that have helped them significantly in getting funding. We often tell companies that receiving SBIR funding allows them to avoid having to seek venture capital money, but it also helps them attract venture capital if additional funding is needed. These companies are doing some of the early stage science that will show if the technology is practical or not. They have to look at how it's going to be commercialized, and in taking these steps, the company is reducing the risk, both the technological risk and the market risk that a venture capital firm would be looking at. And the VC can also view this as a due diligence process. In other words, if a company's technology has been validated by scientists within a federal agency, the VC has some assurance that there is some merit behind it.

Q: Do you have tips or suggestions for a prospective company that wants to go down this path; advice that you've seen other businesses follow that have made them successful in securing these types of grants?

A: Persistence would be one thing. As I mentioned, only one in seven proposals is accepted. Now many of those proposals shouldn't be accepted. They're really not good proposals. What we've seen is about 1 in 3 good proposals gets funded so just because your one has been rejected, you shouldn't let that dishearten you too much. Stay after it. I know of an entrepreneur who submitted 8 proposals that were all rejected before he finally got a proposal that was accepted. This business has since gone on to receive millions of dollars in SBIR funding to assist with the company's R&D efforts. So persistence is necessary. Also, do not be afraid to seek out help. It is an area where some guidance can be very valuable to the company, and if you try to do it all yourself and you are new to the process you are going to miss a lot.

Q: This has been a very informative discussion and your comments will be helpful for people looking into the programs. Do you have suggestions for where our readers should go to find more in-depth information about these programs?

A: First you can go to the SBIR Assistance Program website, www.innovate.gatech.edu/sbir. Other good websites for information are www.zyn.com/sbir and www.sbirworld.com.

CHAPTER 4

Lori Whitted, General Partner
Atlanta Life Venture Fund

Whitted has a wealth of start-up, public company, consulting, and private equity experience. Prior to the Atlanta Life Venture Fund, she was a General Partner with Venturepreneur where her investment focus was early-stage applied technology companies, with particular emphasis on telecommunications, Internet, VoIP and enterprise software technologies. Prior to that role, Whitted was Vice President of e-Commerce at Worldspan, a director of corporate development at The Washington Post Company and later Vice President at The WashingtonPost.com. Whitted was a co-founder of The McLean Group, a private investment bank. She was also a co-founder of Image Café and facilitated the sale of this venture-backed company to Network Solutions, joining that firm following the sale. Whitted spent the first six years of her career as a financial manager for GE Capital and at First Union National Bank. After completing Harvard Business School with an MBA in 1992, she joined the Boston Consulting Group. Whitted also holds an undergraduate degree in economics with a minor in biomedical engineering from Duke University, where she was an A.B. Duke Scholar.

Q: The Atlanta Life Venture Fund is a new endeavor at the time of this interview. Would you give our readers some of the background that led to the creation of this new fund?

A: Atlanta Life is a 100 plus year old financial institution that was founded by an African American, Alonzo Herndon. In early 2007, Atlanta Life acquired the late Maynard Jackson's firm, Jackson Securities. Jackson is the fourth largest African American owned financial institution in the United States. In talking to the president of Atlanta Life a couple of years ago when I was out doing some fundraising for Venturepreneur Parnters, my prior fund, I learned that Atlanta Life had moved into financial services in a much broader way. They had realized there was a need in the marketplace for a venture fund that focused on minority entrepreneurs. I could understand their desire for such a fund as I had seen firsthand the difficulty minorities in particular face as they attempt to get access to early stage and growth capital. This fund was started basically to address that need as well as the need of Fortune 1000 companies trying to expand their base of minority suppliers. These larger corporations have a desire to work with minority suppliers but often find that the suppliers are not of a large enough scale. This fund will be working with Fortune 1000 companies to identify and assist exceptional minority suppliers with their expansion plans. So again, the fund was started out of a need recognized by two very large financial services companies that target African Americans.

Q: You talked about the fund focusing on the minority community, but is there a particular investment philosophy that will set it apart from other funds in the market?

A: Well again, just the focus on minority entrepreneurs sets it apart in many ways because to my knowledge there are probably only two other funds in the United States that have this as even a part of their focus. Our investment philosophy will be to have a balanced portfolio by focusing on three types of companies. We will provide growth capital for existing minority enterprises that have more than $1 million in revenue. Secondly, we will look at some early stage deals where very experienced minority entrepreneurs are attacking large markets with an innovative and defensible offering. Lastly, we will be looking at majority-owned companies as potential acquisition targets where we can then place a minority team inside those companies and turn them into a robust minority enterprise.

Q: What types of companies are you looking to invest in? Are there particular industry segments, for example, that you will be focusing on?

A: No, there really aren't. Because we've narrowed the market by geography – the Southeast primarily and by the fact that we're looking primarily at minority entrepreneurs, we think that that's probably narrow enough and that if we narrow it anymore then it is going to be difficult to find an attractive pool of candidates.

Q: Why do you think this segment of the market as been so under served by existing companies in the business of providing capital?

A: The reality is that there have been a number of studies that talk about the disparity in available capital for minority enterprises. A number of government studies as well as studies done in private equity have documented this. Why it is underserved I think is due probably to two reasons. One, we all know is that: "it's not so much what you know as it is who you know." There's just not enough ongoing or casual interaction between gifted minority entrepreneurs and the individuals who control large pools of private equity capital. I think there's also a lack of experience, a lack of knowledge for some of these entrepreneurs in terms of how to go about raising money. I co-founded a company called Image Café in early 1998. I remember going out trying to raise money for that company. At the time, I was CEO of the company and we went to all of the well known VCs that did early stage investing in the Northern Virginia area. We would get through initial meetings, and then couldn't push through to a term sheet and I couldn't quite figure out why we couldn't push through. We wound up raising $750,000 in friends, family and angel money. We never got the institutional

VC though some started to look at the company eventually, but 18 months later we sold the company for $21 million. It was clearly a good idea, it was clearly a concept at the time that venture capital should have backed, but because my partner and I didn't necessarily have the contacts – it was our first time out and we were both young – we just couldn't crack the nut. In the Southeast in particular, there was a lack of venture capital for anybody. When you add gender and ethnicity to the mix, you get those two things going together with the geographic shortcomings and it just compounds the problems.

Q: How much money will be allocated to this fund and what type of investments by size are you planning to make?

A: The fund will max at $40 million, but we're targeting $25 million for the start of the fund. The type of business and its development stage will determine the size of the investment. This will be a co-investment fund, let me emphasize that. We will not be the lead investors. So, for growth capital we would probably be looking to put in $2 million to $3 million. For early stage companies; $1.5 million max at least for the first two rounds. Obviously, we will reserve follow-on capital to protect our position in promising portfolio companies, but those would be the size of our initial positions. As for acquisitions, it depends upon the size of the deal, but again it's a co-investment fund, so we look at our stake as probably being 20 percent of the capital being provided.

Q: What type of company will you be considering at the idea stage versus the type of company that you would be looking at that may be further down the line and already generating revenue?

A: At the idea stage, again because of the size of the fund that we have, we would be looking for companies that are capital efficient. They need to be addressing a large market obviously, and they need to be led by seasoned entrepreneurs. We are not likely to invest in a first time entrepreneur. And when I say capital efficient, I'm describing a company that on $3 million or less can get to a point in three years or less where it's either a good acquisition target or there is some other exit possibility. So, essentially we're talking about software companies. That's really what fits that type of description. Services companies are hard to monetize. Production oriented companies require much more infrastructure. It's most likely going to be some sort of software or Internet based company that will attract our early stage investment capital.

Q: By starting a new fund, you are indicating that you see an opportunity to achieve the type of returns venture investments are known for. How do you view the market situation overall as we near the close of the decade, and are you comfortable with the return expectations?

A: Yes we are looking to have venture returns, but our limited partners are most likely corporations, so in terms of our investments in suppliers to Fortune 1000 companies, our LPs will get not only a monetary return from the fund – the typical financial return – but they will also be getting a strategic return. Part of our strategy with this fund is to serve dual purposes, so if we don't get a 30%+ return that will not be considered bad for our LPs because going into it they are looking for a stable, less risky investments and a double bottom line. Even though it's a venture fund, we're not focused on finding one big home run. We're looking for the majority of our companies to give a positive 3x to 6x return over a 3- to 5-year horizon. That's a slightly different strategy from a lot of funds. In terms of the market, there is a lot of money out there. Balanced funds with a disciplined and conservative approach to venture investing are not having a hard time raising capital right now. There has been money sitting on the sidelines for quite a while. I think that after the 2008 election, everything in the economy is going to pick up regardless of which way the election goes. I think there has been a lot of uncertainty among Americans in general and especially in the financial markets that will be settle out after the elections. So, I anticipate that the next ten years while they won't return to the frothy periods of the mid to late nineties, I think it's going to be a very healthy market, and one that will do well for private equity over that period.

Q: Explain a little more about the exit strategies you were referring to earlier. You mentioned the potential acquisition of your target companies, but is there a possibility that some of the companies you are considering would be able to do a public stock offering?

A: The fact of the matter is that the most common exit for any venture backed company is an acquisition – and for an early growth stage company it would be considered a micro acquisition, which is an acquisition under $50 million. This is the most likely exit for those companies. Because of the amount of capital that we're looking to put in and the structure of the deal, we still believe we can get a pretty nice return out of a capital efficient early stage company that goes out for $50 million or less in 3 to 5 years. We are also considering creation of holding company or other platform company to acquire not only some of the companies that we might fund but other companies as well and then take that larger company public. We will continue to evaluate that strategy as we move through the market.

Q: When you are evaluating ideas and evaluating the entrepreneur that is presenting an idea to you, what will this entrepreneur have to bring to your attention to get you excited?

A: Well first of all they better believe in it and it better be obvious that they believe in it. I want to see substantial personal skin in the game because they're the ones that have to get up everyday and make this thing work. I like to see entrepreneurs significantly personally invest both emotionally and financially into their idea. That's first and foremost. Secondly, they need to have a business plan that makes sense in terms of the current market environment. Beyond a personal investment and the idea itself, they must have a team that is investment worthy. The team must be well-led and each member must be credible in his or her role. Because markets change, ideas may turn out not to be as viable as you thought, but a good solid team can often turn the corner and make a strategy work in a changing environment. They can adapt the strategy and can do whatever needs to be done to protect the investors' capital and make a potentially bad deal go well. I've been involved personally with enough entrepreneurial ventures to understand that if you don't have a team that is flexible, persistent, knowledgeable and completely committed, it doesn't matter how good the business plan is. It doesn't matter what the market is; it's all about execution and steadfastness to making something positive happen.

Q: How do you view your fund's role in the ongoing management of a business receiving an investment? Will you have a board seat or will there be some other type of arrangement in terms of the management structure?

A: It will be deal by deal as to whether or not we have a board seat because we are a co-investment fund. To some extent our board presence will depend upon the size of our investment relative to the other investors, but we certainly will have an active oversight role. Even if we don't have a board seat, we will seek observation rights. I don't like to use the word management as it relates to our role on the team because if I've got to manage the company then we've got the wrong team in place. But we do bring a substantial amount of practical real world experience to an entrepreneur, and so we would expect that they would be open to input and suggestions from us as partners.

Q: You have an interesting background in the venture capital market that provides different perspectives – from a corporate perspective, from a VC perspective and from being an entrepreneur in your own right. What has been your most interesting experience in venture investing?

A: My most interesting experience has been watching an online company evolve through multiple strategies, and seeing the CEO carry on when all other entrepreneurs I think would have given up. The way they've been able to structurally make it work for the investors by changing the terms of the deal; to see this entrepreneur do whatever has been necessary to survive. If someone had asked me even six months ago if I thought the company would survive, I would have said no, they are out of cash. I invested in the company at seed stage and again when they needed another bridge. I've known the CEO for years and we co-founded a prior company together. I've watched him sell personal property and do whatever it took to make it work. I think that's probably been my most interesting experience; working with the investors, working with that entrepreneur, just watching him stick to it has turned into a good experience. I actually think he'll probably sell that company within twelve months for a very, very, very handsome return. Like I said, it's all about the people. His idea didn't hit me as earth shattering, but some people have a way of creating entrepreneurial magic. So that's probably one of my more interesting stories from a human as well as from an investment perspective.

Q: That's a great example of a positive experience; do you have a negative experience that would be enlightening to entrepreneurs reading this?

A: This is probably more from an entrepreneur's perspective as opposed to from a venture capitalist perspective, but I think this is a helpful story for both. I was an officer in a start-up company in the mid to late nineties. We went out and raised a half million dollars from friends and family and came back and raised a first round of institutional capital. We made the decision to take most of that capital and put it in support of a partnership with a very large corporation because the CEO was convinced that the corporation was going to acquire the company. In fact, the corporation had said as much. There was a gentlemen's handshake and even some documentation to support it. So, we took the vast majority of that institutional capital and put it to work supporting this large partner. Well guess what? That public company had a large investor and board member that had a competing product and when they got wind of the fact that this company had a strategic partnership with our company, they applied pressure for a change. So at the eleventh hour, two weeks before our launch, our partner pulled out of the co-branded partnership and there we were, this little bitty company with nowhere to turn. We had gone out on the press tour, the partnership launch was in magazines, the screen shot of our product with the co-branded logo publicized everywhere, but the deal was dead. We never recovered. We simply could not raise a third round of capital in time. The market went cold for about 6 months and those were the 6 months right after the failed partnership. We had spent essentially all of the money in support of this partner. The moral of the story is when you're a mouse; don't get that close to any one elephant. We ended up having to sell the technology assets of the company in a fire sale to another public company and move on. That was probably my biggest learning experience. For a small company, it's very easy to be attracted to a big public company as a partner and to think that "gosh, this is our meal ticket." But in reality, a small startup is for the most part not even on the radar screen of the big public company. The big company went on and it was no big deal, but its decisions literally took our company out.

Q: Your advice to entrepreneurs based on that experience, then, would be to spread your risks and to avoid depending too greatly on one customer?

A: To spread your risk, yes. But in thinking about the venture investors that we had, we could have received better advice. I learned something in terms of the guidance – the board guidance given the company. The venture investors that we had at that point were so enamored with the idea of having this large public company cozy up to us that they too had bought into the whole notion and they were counting the money before the deal was even complete. So as an investor, I am very, very wary of any company that is overly dependent upon any one partnership or supplier.

Q: When an entrepreneur approaches you with an idea, how important is having a formal business plan prepared?

A: Very important. I want to see something in writing. My experience in the past has been that we've gotten inundated with requests for meetings, so my first step in the screening process is a request that they send me a business plan, at least an executive summary of the plan. It tells me how organized and serious the entrepreneur is. I also want to see how well he or she communicates in writing. I don't like plans written by consultants and they are usually easy to spot. Quite often the business plan is going to be the first point of entry into a discussion with us, so if you haven't taken the time to research the market and come up with a credible plan that you can put down on paper, then I have no reason to think that I want to give you my time or my investors' money.

Q: How important are financial projections as part of the business plan? Are you more interested in understanding the entrepreneur's knowledge of the market or the financial projections?

A: Financial projections are important. Yes, it's an important discipline. You need to do it; you need to show me how much money you need and that you understand what you are going to do with that money. If you tell me you're going to go from zero customers to 10 million in two years, then I'm probably going to know that you have no experience in the real world because it just doesn't happen that way. It allows me to evaluate just how sophisticated and experienced that person is in terms of judging reality. A person might have a great idea; might be very personable, but if they don't understand the realities of how their business is going to work, then they won't get an investment from us. Businesses are all about creating shareholder value. Financials are my only way of evaluating a company's potential to deliver acceptable returns to my shareholders.

CHAPTER 5

Wright Steenrod, Principal
Chrysalis Ventures

Steenrod joined Chrysalis in June 2001 and was promoted to Principal in 2005. At Chrysalis, Steenrod has worked with Ygnition, Genscape, and Appriss, among others. He focuses on media and communications. Prior to Chrysalis, Steenrod was Vice President of Business Development for Darwin Networks, a former Chrysalis portfolio company. From 1995 to 1998, he worked at SunTrust Bank in Atlanta as an Associate in Mergers & Acquisitions. Prior to SunTrust, he served five years in the U.S. Marine Corps from which he was honorably discharged as Captain. Wright has a B.A. in Economics from Princeton University. A Louisville native, Wright is active in the community working with organizations such as the Kentuckiana Boys and Girls Clubs. He serves as a member of the Entrepreneurship Council at the University of Louisville's College of Business and Public Affairs.

Q: Chrysalis Ventures takes its name from the process of a caterpillar morphing into a butterfly. Would you please elaborate on your firm's philosophy and what this symbolism means?

A: Chrysalis' philosophy is to invest in early stage companies and the reason that we have the caterpillar morphing into the butterfly is that we like to identify companies when – like the caterpillar – they are not particularly attractive or dynamic. We have the ability to recognize potential in businesses that can still be very early in their life cycle and build around it with money, experience and advice. And, we nurture what was the caterpillar through its initial growth stages and then as it matures into a butterfly that symbolizes the process of selling the company on to bigger players or into the public market.

Q: You joined Chrysalis according to your biography, in 2001; that had to be an interesting time to join a venture capital firm. What led you to the profession at a time when there was so much turmoil in the capital markets?

A: I like being involved with companies at the earlier stages of their growth when you are still working with a business model that is not yet fully determined and you are involved in figuring it out. I enjoyed working in early stage companies. Now, it is satisfying to work at it from the investor side. I think the timing for someone like me, early in their venture career, couldn't have been better. There were a lot of broad lessons that people learned in the bubble, but lessons aside, most of those deals – as everyone knows now – didn't work out. So, financially it was not the best time to be in the venture business. Joining the industry right after that – when it was in a down cycle, may turn out to be the best timing because I think the returns are going to be better.

Q: How do you compare the climate for venture funding then to the climate that you see now?

A: Compared to 2001, from a national and global perspective there is a whole lot more money looking to invest in companies. In 2001, a great number of firms were licking their wounds. I think regionally, there is more activity than there was in 2001. But we have seen some funds that raised their first fund in 1999 and 2000 – and invested that that money over the course of the next five years – found themselves in 2005 and 2006 struggling to raise money for new funds. They are finding it difficult to remain in business. So, my perspective is there is more money available than in 2001 but less than in 2004.

Q: When you are looking back to the early part of the decade, what do you think were the important lessons that venture firms learned that has changed the way the market operates now?

A: I think everybody is wary of investing into hysteria. My personal opinion would be that a lot of folks still blame the bubble bursting upon particular management teams getting over extended. I tend to think that when you look at an industry like telecommunications where nearly every deal got wiped out regardless of the management team, I don't think that you can say that's a management issue. I think that's a sector where venture firms were as guilty as anybody else. They were looking at the investment banker saying these are companies you can take public in the next six to twelve months. The companies were getting funded with a business plan of going public and when the public market turned in 2000, the business plans didn't have anything to stand on. And so, I think people are a little bit more wary of hysteria, but with that said I'm not sure what would happen if the public market opened up again like they were in the last part of the 1990s.

Q: Do you believe any of that has translated into the types of businesses that receive venture funding today?

A: That was a time when anything associated with the Internet was getting funding. I think there is more focus now; there's more attention paid to the business model and creating strategic advantage with your business plan that will result in somebody acquiring you. I think probably those businesses that are getting funded today are getting funded with the idea that they will sell to a private equity firm or to a strategic acquirer as opposed to going public.

Q: Chrysalis has said that it prefers to invest in what it described as the "under-ventured" Midwest and South. Why do you think these regions have been under served from a venture perspective?

A: The venture industry itself is not all that old and I think where it started in Silicon Valley and in Boston would still be the two major centers. It's easier for people to invest around what they know and in the geographic areas they know. It is easier for people to do a deal down the street rather than travel across time zones to find it. And I think it's more challenging for someone that's not in the region because we cover something like 23 states and travel a good deal to find deals. But, there's a lot of research dollars that gets poured into the Midwest and Southeast and there are a lot of companies in the Midwest and Southeast that are going to appear on Inc. magazine's list of the 500 fastest growing companies. There is a lot of business activity out here, but it is spread over a much larger region, which makes it challenging for somebody without our regional network of connections to get their hands around.

Q: How would you describe the deal flow coming out of these regions? By these regions I mean the Midwest and the South.

A: I would say for our deal flow, it's never been better.

Q: Your firm specializes in technology, healthcare, media and communications. What about these sectors are particularly attractive to you?

A: The firm has been around since 1993 and has had a lot of success since then by specializing in companies that fit under an umbrella term that we call technology-enabled business services. We're not an investor that's going to invest in technology development per se; we're not going to define what goes into the next piece of telecom hardware. We do think we can identify businesses and identify teams that are taking emerging technologies and applying business service models around them. Healthcare, media and communications are the areas where we feel our experience and our networks are the strongest and we believe these industries are promising sectors with a lot of wind at their backs.

Q: A follow up question to that. Your company's website excludes biotechnology from healthcare. Why is biotechnology looked at as a different sector?

A: Because you have to have a good deal of technical expertise to evaluate it, particularly in the drug discovery part of the life science business. I think the medical device business is very competitive and we continue to look into exploring some of those life science investments but I think overall, especially on the drug discovery type investment, they tend to be pretty capital intensive and you have got to hold them for a long time and we're just not attracted to that model.

Q: Chrysalis talks about choosing its investments based largely on strong management teams. How do you go about evaluating the strengths and weaknesses of a management team? By that I mean, do you do some type of a formal analysis or is this a decision driven by gut-feelings?

A: All management decisions have a component of gut feelings about them. I mean do you feel comfortable with the people; do they have high integrity; do they do what they say they are going to do; do they have the experience necessary to do it? These are the kind of questions we ask when evaluating a management team. So, yes there's a gut feeling you get when answering those questions. We also rely a lot on reference checks and background checks. A large majority of the entrepreneurs are folks that we know, or came to us through a warm introduction. We actually do have some personality behavioral tools we use to evaluate individuals to a degree, but more often we use those tools to evaluate teams to gain insight into how certain teams are going to react to certain situations and how teams behave. We want to understand the team dynamic.

Q: If management is such a key factor in your decision process, what would you tell an entrepreneur is the one thing they should do before they contact your firm in order to make a good first impression?

A: I would say for all entrepreneurs that having a warm introduction would help immensely. Because, whenever anybody walks in the door, the first thing before you understand what their product is or what their business model is, you want to get some gut feel for how credible they are, that they actually know what they're talking about and have the ability to deliver. Having someone we know make that introduction is important. It speaks to the entrepreneur's networking ability. I think it helps us evaluate what kind of sales story they have. Just like when you are funded and selling your product. You know cold calling works, but having that network that gives you warm introductions, at least makes that introductory call easier. I think probably the same goes for us.

Q: Do you find today's entrepreneur to be savvy about raising capital? Or, do you find yourself having to do a lot of education about the process?

A: Oh, I think they are savvier. I think probably when I joined there were still a lot of entrepreneurs that did not realize that the boom was over. They were expecting business plans to get funded that had no operations established or customers or anything like that and they still had very high valuation expectations. I find that the entrepreneurs today are savvier about the whole thing.

Q: You just mentioned valuations and that is the subject of my next question. Do you think that today's entrepreneurs have expectations about valuations that are more aligned with market realities?

A: I do. I think entrepreneurs are now more part of a funding eco system. Most of the entrepreneurs we deal with have gone through a valuation process as part of an angel round of investment. Angel investors are part of that eco system and it is now better established. But we still see deals where an entrepreneur has been able to raise $1 million at a $20 million valuation and they come into the venture market with maybe a part of a product developed and a beta customer and expect the venture market to invest at a premium to what the angel investment was, and that is not realistic.

Q: But do you find that to be more of the exception to the rule?

A: I would say yes.

Q: Chrysalis takes an active role in the management of its portfolio companies. Is this normally through a board seat, or through some other formal reporting structure?

A: People ask if we are active investors and I always say that yes we are considered an active investor. By that I mean we are going to take a board seat and we'll want to be involved in key decisions the company makes. And there are three areas of decisions that we want to have a say in: the hiring of key personnel, how the company raises debt and/or equity, and strategy. We want to have an advisory role in the business; we're not going to dictate to management, but we want it to be a collaborative process. As far as the reporting goes, we actually have what we call our board expectation package which talks about monthly reporting and suggests the format by which portfolio companies can report not just the financial results but also give a written feel for what's going on in the business over the past month. We find that by using these tools, when we have board meetings, the meetings are not focused around what the company did the last month but allows the board to be more strategically oriented.

Q: Is this hands-on approach expected by the entrepreneurs seeking capital, or do you find that this can be a source of tension that you have to work through?

A: I think entrepreneurs expect a hands on approach and we generally work through that and explain that pretty well up front so I would not say there's any tension that has to be worked through. I think dealing with an executive that basically says I just want your money and I don't want your advice is a negative sign for us and somebody we would not invest with. Venture firms can open doors for folks but we're not going to close the deal. We can introduce an entrepreneur to people but he's still got to get in and close it. The managers of our portfolio companies are the ones who make the day-to-day decisions for running the business; they are the key decision makers on budgets and sales calls. We can open doors and we can help sort through some of those process roadblocks, but at the end of the day the company has to have internal processes and strong management running those processes to be successful.

Q: Please describe some of the deals that you are currently evaluating in terms of deal stage and the size of the investment you are looking to make. Give the entrepreneurs reading this book a flavor of the kind of deals that you do.

A: The first point is that we are a technology enabled services investor in the Midwest and Southeast. As a technology enabled services investor we are not investing in the next great widget or the next great drug or the next great medical device. We don't want to invest in intellectual property per se although IP is an important part of building a services business; we want a service business model. And, within that then we can look pretty broadly and pretty opportunistically with the focus on healthcare and media and communications. In healthcare the general premise is that costs cannot keep rising at the rate they are rising because they will break the system and economy at some point. With costs up 20% year to year the healthcare system has to be made more productive. Fortunately, the same information technology tools that have made every other industry more productive are now starting to find proven models in making healthcare more productive. So businesses that can capitalize on this trend are very attractive to us. On the media side, we look at media not necessarily as old media or new media, but as media in general. Within media we focus on business to business information services, ad supported lead generation businesses, and enabling technologies that improve media businesses. An enabling technology example is software that effectively inserts advertising in a video. On the communication side, we target "managed services" businesses that generate recurring revenue. We look for those businesses in niches where we think the companies have competitive advantages.

Q: In terms of the stage of these companies, would these companies need to be generating revenue in order to get your attention?

A: Yes. We will do some seed deals which we consider investing in a company pre-revenue, but the large majority of our deals will be early stage meaning the company has a product and they have some customers and some revenue. There's no rule but $500,000 to $2 million annual revenue or more is what we like to see. From a due diligence perspective, it allows us to evaluate that the product works and somebody is buying it. At this level of revenue there are enough customers we can talk to so we can understand why they bought it; understand what other options they looked at so we can understand the competitive dynamic.

Q: What size of investments do you make in a company?

A: We're going to look to make an investment somewhere between $2 million to $4 million up front in the company; and look to get $12 million into the company over the life of the investment.

Q: You mentioned earlier that you often co-invest with other institutions. Could you explain the process of co-investing? What is the strategy behind that for you as an investment company and what might that mean for the company receiving the funding?

A: We co-invest with others and then we do a number of deals where we're the sole investor. It comes down to where we think we would want to have an investor with different experience on board or where the capital need of the company is great enough that we need another investor. Like for a $7 million round; we are not going to do $7 million. Our fund is not big enough to invest $7 million in an early stage company by ourselves because we want to have reserves to fall back on in an investment, so we would go find a partner to split the deal with us. As an entrepreneur you want to know that you have the best set of advisors around the table and have enough capital to fund a business plan and also with the knowledge that things always take longer and usually take a little bit more money than everybody expects. So you want your investors to have sufficient reserves to probably give you a little bit more money over time than you think you might need. And I think from the entrepreneur's perspective, the only plus to having one venture investor is that it makes your life easier. That's your funding source and your advice source and it's going to be easy to manage. I think the downside is if you only have one set of advisors and if that particular investor sours on the deal; if things don't go well, you're stuck with finding a new set of investors. A syndicate offers you a broader pool of advice and it diversifies your capital sources. Depending on what you think your company needs, between one and three investors make sense. But if you have a syndicate that has six investors and they have not all worked together before then you don't know how it's going to turn out. Sometimes managing that syndicate takes time because there will be personality conflicts and differences of opinion. The sources of capital should be chosen carefully because when you are managing conflicts within your venture syndicate you're not adding value to your business.

Q: Taking a look at some investments that you have been involved in, what would you describe as the characteristics of a successful investment?

A: A successful investments represents the combination of market opportunity with the right management team. Management teams that can grow and adapt with the market opportunity are very important to success. It means working with intelligent, flexible people who can adapt to the market as it changes.

Q: Conversely, what are the characteristics of a failed deal and what lessons came out of that that may be enlightening for entrepreneurs?

A: It's primarily about failing to develop a customer base. A set of customers were willing to buy the product but not enough to really validate the model, so the model never works. There are times when probably the main reason for failure is management. This often happens when the management was better at selling than executing. They could paint a great picture, but couldn't really execute to the picture, and didn't have the hiring skills necessary to build the team around them that could execute. And so you are left with a business that has promise, but it just never takes off.

Q: Is there anything you want to add to this discussion; a piece of final advice for the entrepreneur reading this?

A: I've never read a formal study of it, but I think if you go look at the history of successful entrepreneurs, a lot of entrepreneurs that made a lot of money and retained a lot of ownership in their business had a business that was doing pretty well before they went to seek venture capital. You think about Amazon.com, which had revenue when Kleiner Perkins invested in them, and even Google was generating millions of visitors a month. The marketplace was validating these companies before they sought venture funding. A lot of entrepreneurs think that venture capital is still "start up idea" funding and see venture capital as the first option. Entrepreneurs would be better served, both in terms of how they spend their time and by the kind of valuation they would get, by focusing on raising friends and family money, building the business and giving us something that is tangible to look at as opposed to just putting something up on a white board and going out and trying to raise money off of it. That no longer works.

CHAPTER 6

Charles D. Moseley
General Partner
Noro-Moseley Partners

Moseley led the founding of Noro-Moseley Partners in 1983, an Atlanta-based venture firm that has invested in more than 160 businesses since its inception. Prior to forming Noro-Moseley Partners, Moseley was a Senior Vice President and Director of The Robinson-Humphrey Company, Inc., a major regional investment banking firm in Atlanta, Georgia. He joined the Corporate Finance Department in 1968 and became its Director in 1976. Under his management, this department grew to become the leading corporate investment banking operation in the Southeast. His corporate finance activities included managing public offerings of debt and equity, private placements of debt and venture capital, mergers and acquisitions, valuations, and financial consulting. In 1982, Robinson-Humphrey was acquired by American Express and is now a subsidiary of SunTrust. Moseley received a Bachelor of Industrial Engineering degree from the Georgia Institute of Technology and an MBA degree from Harvard Business School.

Q: You formed Noro-Moseley Partners in 1983. What led you into the venture capital business at that time?

A: I was the manager of the corporate finance business at Robinson-Humphrey and we had done several financings – both private and public – for three companies where venture funds came in and invested in those companies from outside the area. These three companies – Management Science America (MSA), HBO & Co. and Intergraph – were great technology companies. They were homegrown, but there was nobody around the Southeast with institutional money to finance those businesses. So, in the process of helping bring venture funds into those companies, I saw the world of venture capital; saw that there was a need here. When Robinson-Humphrey was sold in 1982 to American Express, it presented a good opportunity for me to leave and start this.

Q: How do you view the overall state of the market for venture funding; and in answering that, please consider it from the perspective of raising money as well the number of deals that are available for investment?

A: To put the current market in perspective, let's look at the last several years. With the Internet bubble of 2000, there was also a bubble in the amount of money raised in the venture capital business in the U.S. At that time – 1999 and 2000 – it was very easy to raise venture capital and there were historic amounts raised. After that – on the down slope of the bubble – it became increasingly difficult to raise venture capital. And the amount of money going into the venture business declined significantly – back to what would be considered more normal levels. So, if you take out the bubble, the market now looks like it did in the 90s before the bubble, and that has been the case for the last few years. I believe, however, that the market for raising venture capital remains difficult except for the established funds. Everybody wants to invest in the top 5 percent or 10 percent of venture funds, and of course, that leaves out 95 percent of the venture firms who are struggling to raise new funds. We have been very fortunate in that we just completed raising our 6th fund which is in excess of $100 million. It is probably the largest venture fund that has been raised in the last 12 months in our territory. On the other side of the coin, because money is difficult for the funds to raise, it's also a little bit more of a scarce commodity for companies to get. Therefore, I believe it's going to turn out to be a good time to invest money in companies, just because of the law of supply and demand. The quality of the deals that are available is improving. But the volume of those deals is no where near what they were back at the peak. Then everybody wanted to be a venture capitalist or an entrepreneur, but when reality set in and they learned that it's not so much fun being on the down slope, the number of people looking to raise money in startup companies thinned out considerably. We are beginning to see that pick up now.

Q: Your firm has always had a geographic focus on the Southeast. What about this region has been attractive to you from an investment perspective?

A: First and foremost, it is what we know. We are all from this area, we were raised here, we went to school – at least undergraduate here – we worked here and saw what was going on in the territory. I think it has been underfinanced. The Southeast has always been capital poor and it really continues to remain so today compared to the centers that you would compare us to, the Northeast, the West Coast and to some extent, Texas. We are beginning to see a lot of exciting developments in the Southeast anchored around the same kinds of things that gauged the start of venture capital in other parts of the country. In the Northeast it was centered on education of MIT and Harvard in the Boston 128 Corridor. On the West Coast it is clear that Stanford, Cal Berkley and Cal Tech played central roles in the establishment of the technology industry there. Here in the Southeast – even though it is maybe 20 or 30 years behind – we're seeing activity around the region's technology educational centers, particularly around Georgia Tech in Georgia and the research triangle in North Carolina with Duke, UNC and NC State. You have to have engineering and computer science graduates to have technology companies and these places turn them out. As the influence of these technology universities continues to grow, they will spawn more companies over the years.

Q: Speaking geographically, is it easier for entrepreneurs on the West Coast – in Silicon Valley especially – to raise capital?

A: I think that that's probably true. Silicon Valley is a very small territory, and there is a large amount of venture capital there and a large number of technology firms located there. That sort of melting pot really spawns economic development and entrepreneurial ideas. I believe it would be clear that it would be easier to do it out there. By the same token, it should be easier to stand out here. If you have the next greatest thing and you are able to get it going, it will be pretty apparent in our territory that you have something special. There will be less competition for funding.

Q: When you were getting your start, you talked about funds from other areas coming into the Southeast to do deals. How willing are firms from the West Coast and the Northeast to do deals outside of their regions today?

A: Everybody will always go somewhere where there is a great deal, so there is money in every region from every other region. But it's really difficult to monitor and help your companies from a long way off. Therefore, when a firm from another region does a deal here, they like to have local co-investors. We have been pretty successful in attracting those kinds of co-investors into some of the deals that we have. Venture business is a hands on business and if you are on the West Coast and you have to take two days out of your week to attend a two-hour meeting, it becomes pretty difficult. So, without question, geography plays a role in investment decisions.

Q: You were talking earlier about the Internet bubble of 2000. Did that permanently alter the landscape for venture funding, or have you seen it return to the way it was before that period?

A: I'm not sure we'll ever see – ever is a long time, but not in any near term – a return to the way it was during that period. It was so incredibly *more* in every measure than it had been before. The volume of deals, number of IPOs, numbers of companies getting financed; it was many multiples of what it was before and after, so it truly was a bubble. Even today with a strong rebound in the stock market, NASDAQ is half of what it was in 2000, so you can imagine how much difference there was in the market at that time. But I don't think that it permanently altered the landscape of venture financing. When it floated back down, it put a number of firms out of business. But the overall market for venture financing is now coming back. I think 10 to 15 years from now, that period in the market will be looked at exactly the way it is now; it was a bubble.

Q: How about the entrepreneurs? Have they changed since that time; is there more of a realistic approach to the capital raising process now?

A: You know there is, but I don't know that this is good. There are fewer entrepreneurs stepping out to do something today than there were in those times. The market is more selective about what kinds of companies get financed, so from the entrepreneurs' perspective, it's tougher. Certainly, from the investors' side it may be a more realistic situation to deal in.

Q: At what stage of a company's development are you investing; what are you looking for at that stage?

A: We concentrate on established companies with growth prospects, as opposed to two other ends of the spectrum – a really true start up where somebody has an idea and wants to describe what their idea is and the leveraged buy out of some large established division of some company. We concentrate in the middle. The typical company we look for would be one that has $5 million to $50 million of revenue. It would have a lot of growth opportunities, and present an opportunity for us to be the first institutional investor. The company would be owned primarily by the individuals who started it. There might be some outside individual money beyond the owners, but probably not another venture fund yet unless it was a smaller venture fund. That would be the typical picture for us.

Q: How much of an investment would normally be made in such a company?

A: We want to make sure we are properly reserved to take care of how much we expect a company will need over the life of the investment, which for us generally stands anywhere from four years to seven years. During that time, we typically end up doubling our investment in the company. So we might start out investing $2 million to $4 million and ultimately wind up between $5 million and $10 million per company.

Q: What sectors are attracting the most attention from venture investors in general, and then, more specifically, what kinds of companies are you considering?

A: The kinds of companies we are looking at would apply to the general market as well. We describe our interest in four areas. One is information technology, a second would be healthcare products and services, three would be business services, and four is what we call special situations. A special situation would likely be a company in an industry different from what we normally invest in, but probably connected to something we've done in the past. For example, it could be headed by an entrepreneur we've financed in the past. Overall, we are looking for products and services that can be competitive in the marketplaces. In healthcare we look for businesses that make delivering services cheaper, better and more efficient. In business services, we want to find companies that are innovating; that offer products and services to help businesses be more efficient using the information that's so readily available.

Q: Since its inception, your firm has invested in over 160 businesses. I would think that to get to that number, you've also endured 100s if not 1,000s of bad PowerPoint presentations. Could you describe the process you use for evaluating potential investments?

A: It used to be that you got a business plan in the mail; and people thought that the thicker the plan, the better. I think maybe now, people are beginning to understand that a thinner plan might be the better approach. Our deal flow today comes from a variety of sources. It could be direct from an entrepreneur; it could be through an intermediary such as an investment banker, a lawyer, an accountant, or a friend of ours. The first thing we do is to look at the material and decide if it is something that fits what we do. Does it fit into any of the industries or situations that I described? Are they looking for the amount of money at the stage of development that fit the criteria we discussed earlier? If that's the case, then a partner would get in touch with the company to set up a meeting. We would visit the business and pursue it that way. The focal point for our internal processing is a staff meeting held once a week. Everybody sits around and discusses the deals that are on the table – what we've seen and heard. We try to be aggressive ourselves in getting out and talking to people who are in touch with deals so that we are not just sitting back waiting for whatever comes over the transom or through the email. But, we can get bogged down with what comes to us; there's always concern that you are never doing enough prospecting. It's easier to process what you receive, but we feel we need to be out and about to learn about the best possible deals. We do spend a lot of effort on that. Some of our partners have a disproportionate amount of their time devoted to being out prospecting and being in touch with the market place.

Q: You mentioned earlier that a thin business plan maybe better than thick one. Would you elaborate on how important the business plan is to your evaluation process? What should be included?

A: The most important things to us are: what is the business and who are the people involved; what have they done. And that doesn't take a lot of time and effort or a lot of space to describe. We are not interested – at least in the beginning – in all the exhibits and appendices that many include. To really get us interested in a deal doesn't take a lot of volume, but it takes what I just described as being on point. As for projections – everybody is always interested in telling us their projections. Everybody has projections, but most companies don't come close to meeting them. It is not that they are crooked or fraudulent or trying to be deceptive, it's just that the future is uncertain. It is difficult to know what a company is going to be doing three or four years from now, much less what it is going to be doing a year from now. During the course of our diligence, we want to see projections, but the purpose is to really see how they think – not to hold someone to a set of made up numbers. We have to use our own good judgment about relying too much on those.

Q: Would you relate a story about one of your deals that could be enlightening to entrepreneurs about the venture process?

A: There was a company that we looked at that was providing computer support by telephone. This was 10 years ago or so when computers were a little more difficult to use and the software wasn't quite as user friendly. It was really a good idea and the people that were involved were experienced in delivering this kind of help via telephone as opposed to in-house delivery. The targets were big companies. All of what I'm describing is pretty commonplace now, but it wasn't then. The deal went badly, and the primary reason it did was simply timing. The company was a little ahead of its time. My point is that an entrepreneur doesn't get too many swings at the ball, and even if he does everything correctly it still may not work out. Sometimes there's contact with the ball, but it just happens to get hit straight at the third basemen and he's out. Whereas, if the ball were hit just a littlie bit higher, it would have been a game winning single. That's a little bit like the timing with an entrepreneur in a venture deal, as well as with the venture investor. There is a big amount of luck involved, and I think any of us who have been around in the business long enough can recognize that and see either a lucky break or an unlucky break. Timing has a lot to do with success, and an entrepreneur just has to accept that. It was much more difficult – if not impossible – for somebody starting a business in July of 2000 to get funding as opposed to maybe today or maybe July of '97. So, that's purely timing.

Q: In closing, is there one thing you would tell an entrepreneur to do to impress you?

A: Have a really good team of people. Make it look like you are pulling together a culture of knowledgeable people in the business you are in. You get high marks for experience; and putting together an A+ team is very impressive. Some of the best investments we've had have been with people who were simply able to pull together more people like them and build the right culture and instill the right work ethic. Companies must be a collection of people with the right knowledge and experience for what they are trying to do.

CHAPTER 7

John Huntz, Executive Director,
Head of Venture Capital
Arcapita Ventures

Huntz joined Arcapita Ventures in 2005. Prior to joining Arcapita, he worked for the last 14 years at The Fuqua Companies, most recently as Managing Director of Fuqua Ventures. He also served as Executive Vice President and Chief Operating Officer of Fuqua Enterprises, Inc. and Managing Partner of Noble Ventures International. Huntz was also Director of Capital Resources for Arthur Young & Company and was an investment professional at Harrison Capital. He has served as a member of the Board of Directors of the National Venture Capital Association and the Securities and Exchange Commission's Small Business Capital Formation Task Force Executive Committee. Huntz is one of the leaders of the venture community in the Southeast as demonstrated by his founding and leadership of the Atlanta Venture Forum. He is currently Chairman of the Board of Manhattan Associates and also serves on the Board of Directors of Prenova and Alloptic. Huntz received his BBA from Niagara University and holds his MBA from Sacred Heart University.

Q: How do you view the climate for venture investing as we near the end of this decade?

A: As you look at the various cycles we've been in for the last 20 years, it is a very good time. There are plenty of deals and opportunities. We've seen a lot of activity at the upper end of the market with buy-out funds and private equity funds, and in other segments of the market as well. The investor activity I think is going to be very strong for the foreseeable future. There is a lot of liquidity in the market from a variety of sources who are looking for talent to put that money to work for them. Venture investments certainly are one of the asset classes getting strong consideration as evidenced by the amount of funds being raised.

Q: That must translate into a positive situation for companies looking for funding. From an entrepreneur's perspective, do you view this as a good time to engage in the capital raising process?

A: This is a very attractive time simply because there is so much money available. But even with the large amount of capital available, the basic tenants of what venture investors are looking for do not change. Investors are looking for a company that has a strong management team and is addressing a large sustainable market. If you don't have that, it's going to be difficult for you to raise money.

Q: Arcapita is an interesting company; would you please provide some background on your firm?

A: Our mission is to provide innovative and distinct alternative investment opportunities. We aim to generate superior risk-adjusted returns for our investors and strong profitable growth for our shareholders. In our approach to doing business, we embrace the values of originality, integrity, transparency, professional excellence and adherence to an ethical investment policy. We have four total lines of business, corporate investment, real estate investing, asset-based investing, and venture capital as the latest asset class.

Q: How did your U.S. office, which handles the venture investing, come to be based in Atlanta rather than more traditional areas for venture funds such as Silicon Valley or Boston?

A: When the group was being formed about 10 years ago, they looked at investing in the United States, and made a determination that Atlanta was a very attractive place from the overall commerce taking place here, but also for access to travel. It was easy to get anywhere else in the United States from Atlanta. And by opening an office here, we avoided the congestion of a Boston or Silicon Valley. Here, as the new kid on the block, it was much easier to put a flag in the ground and be recognized instantly. It was a move to separate from the noise level that we would have been part of in New York, Boston or the West Coast.

Q: Does having an Atlanta office indicate you have a geographic focus on making investments in the Southeast?

A: Our venture team is headquartered in Atlanta, and we are focused on deals throughout the United States rather than abroad. But we probably end up doing more deals in the Southeast than other regions because we are here, and I personally have been here a long time. I think just the network that we have will facilitate more deals closer to home.

Q: What do you see with other firms; do venture firms typically do more investments closer to their geographic base, or is there a trend toward specializing in an industry or sector without as much regard to geography?

A: I think it varies a lot from fund to fund, but overall, there is more of an industry or sector focus. That is much more the current theme in the way funds are being put together. We're a pretty broad fund, but we consider our sectors to be healthcare, information technology and industrial. We have other buckets, but those three cover our portfolio pretty well.

Q: At what stage in a company's development do you invest; do you look at any pre-revenue companies or are all of your investments in more established businesses?

A: When we set this fund up our partner base wanted to have exposure to growth stage companies. We expect our companies to have their products in the marketplace. We are looking for companies typically that are around $5 million in revenue where we can invest $5 million to $10 million in an initial lead investment and provide the capital for growth. That would be our typical initial investment, and then we'll go up $20 million in a deal.

Q: How do you manage your investments once the money is in? Your website describes Arcapita as active managers of your portfolio companies, but what does that entail?

A: It's been a philosophy of mine since I've been in this business for the past 27 years to be actively engaged at the board level. It is essential for providing guidance and direction more from a strategic standpoint. We want the management team to run the business, but we believe you have to have that active engagement with them to understand what they are doing and to keep the ship in the right lane.

Q: So, you regularly take board positions?

A: In every one of our deals. It's a requirement that we take a board seat.

Q: In considering an investment today, what is your investment horizon, and has that changed over time?

A: With our current fund, which is about a year and a half old, our horizon was 3- to 5 years. We said that at about the sixth year of the fund, we would stop investing and focus our time on what's in the portfolio; stop doing new deals. This also might be the time we want to start planning for a new fund and beginning to do new deals there. As for how the investment horizon has changed historically, I would say that the time horizon has returned to something more normal and reasonable. Back in 1999 and 2000, you were thinking that if you were in a deal more than 18 months you were in it a long time. But that has come back around to a market where 3- to 5 years is not unusual.

Q: You just mentioned 1999 and 2000. At the time, an expected exit strategy was through an initial public offering (IPO), but now a typical exit is through an acquisition. What is your view on the type of exits venture-backed companies should expect in the coming years?

A: I think there will continue to be a situation here and there where an IPO will work. The IPO window opens and closes depending on market conditions. But merger and acquisition – M&A – transactions will be the primary driver of exits.

Q: You mentioned earlier that Arcapita specializes in healthcare and technology. Are there specific types of businesses within those sectors that are particularly attractive to venture investment?

A: In the healthcare sector it is primarily devices and therapeutic care. It's also about managing the data – electronic records management, patient record management and things of that nature.

Q: Is the need to drive costs down in healthcare behind the creation of these kinds of businesses?

A: Well, driving cost down is part of it. But there also is the need to improve the overall quality of patient care, and there is increasing management of the many federal regulations that are coming into play. There are a variety of issues driving the health care sector.

Q: In information technology, what are the trends that are influencing the development of this sector?

A: Basically, I see the Internet as continuing to evolve. We were hearing about Web 2.0 and what that entailed. There is already talk about a version 3.0, so it won't be long before it's going to be 4.0. The young guys we meet understand this; they grew up using this stuff, so it's second hand to them. So I think as the next generation gets involved in utilizing the Internet in different ways, we are going to see dramatic change and that is what's going to be driving the IT part of the market.

Q: As you evaluate the companies you consider for investment, do you put more emphasis on the management team or the underlying business idea?

A: The management team. You can have an A product with a B management team and probably fail. But you can have a B product with an A management and turn the B product into an A product. I believe in the notion that if you have real talent, you have a better chance at success because none of these venture deals are going to go in a straight line. You have to have the capacity to lead a team of people through the maze of pitfalls that you are going to face as an emerging company. The stronger the management team is the better the likelihood that you are going to have a good outcome.

Q: Where do the leaders of your companies come from? Are they serial entrepreneurs or do you have people making successful corporate exits into an entrepreneurial venture?

A: It's a mixture of backgrounds, but I'd say that those who strike out on their own and take a risk are more entrepreneurial to begin with. They tend to grow the business to a certain stage, and then there is a transition to a leadership team with experience really growing businesses. Often, these people have great corporate experience but are also quite entrepreneurial. They see an opportunity and build the team up to go after it. Typically, leaders of our growth-stage companies are more in the latter group.

Q: Are there common mistakes you see entrepreneurs make during the capital raising process that you think others could learn to avoid?

A: From our perspective, I'd say the most common mistakes are overestimating market penetration or revenue growth and underestimating what it is going to cost to get there. Now, I should be really careful calling that a mistake because if the entrepreneur does not have that kind of optimism then he's probably not the right person anyway. But as investors, we are looking for entrepreneurs with the right balance of optimism and reality.

Q: In the role you play in managing your investments, what common piece of advice do you find yourself giving over and over again?

A: I think the most common piece of advice is to 'do it right.' By right – and I don't want to sound overly moralistic about it – but that means approaching relationships with an integrity factor. It means: be up front, play it straight, keep it simple and do what you say you are going to do.

Q: How do you get an early read on all of the issues that are important to you when evaluating a company and its management team?

A: I think the development of the business plan is a key issue. How has the entrepreneur approached it? Did the management team really put the time into developing a plan that makes sense? Does it address all of the components? We look at all these pieces, and the more thorough of a job they have done in preparing their plan and demonstrating to us that they understand the market; the easier it is for us to come to the decision on how we want to invest.

Q: How important are the financial projections in a business plan? Should an entrepreneur spend more time talking about the product and the market or should the emphasis be on the pro formas?

A: The pro formas are just that, they are pro formas and we accept them as projections, but they should be realistic. The stage of company we're looking at should at least have some visibility into what the next couple of years look like and what the effective use of the funds they raise will be. We want to see if they can plausibly tell us what the revenues are going to be and what it will cost to generate that revenue. When we close a deal I give the CEO a T-shirt that says "Happiness is a Positive Cash Flow." Any entrepreneur must keep in mind that a business cannot run without cash coming in the door in excess of what you're spending.

CHAPTER 8

Ted J. Bender III
Managing Director
Croft & Bender

Bender is a co-founder of Croft & Bender, an investment banking firm focused on middle market M&A and private equity transactions. Since its founding in 1996, Croft & Bender has completed over $2.5 billion in M&A advisory transactions and over $700 million in private equity capital raises. In addition, the firm manages two private equity/venture capital funds totaling $44 million. Prior to co-founding Croft & Bender in 1996, Bender was a Managing Director of the Corporate Finance Department at The Robinson-Humphrey Company, Inc. and was a member of its Board of Directors. Bender joined Robinson-Humphrey in 1976, and during his tenure he founded and led several industry practice groups. Bender has been involved in many industries, including general manufacturing, healthcare, software, life sciences, insurance, banking, building materials and business services. Bender has served and continues to serve on the Boards of several corporations. Bender received a B.S. from the University of Alabama in 1971.

Q: To set the stage for our discussion, would you please give an overview of how investment banks fit into the process of raising capital?

A: Investment banks are expected to be experts at all aspects of the process of raising capital or selling a company. This process usually begins with some sort of valuation and moves forward to include evaluating the company's capital markets or strategic alternatives, preparing the company for going to market, and then taking the lead in executing the sales process. This sales or marketing process should be managed so as to generate significant "demand" or interest in the transaction so that the client can be presented with several favorable alternatives. A banker should have experience in both the type of transaction being considered and the client's industry sector.

Q: We're hearing the phrase "private equity" more now. For the entrepreneurs reading this book, would you provide your definition for what that means and how you differentiate private equity from venture capital?

A: The broadest differentiation is that Venture Capital funds invest in early stage companies and Private Equity funds invest in more established companies. Today most venture funds are looking for companies with a "proven business model." Typically, that is a company with some level of customers and revenue. Such companies need capital but they are not able to go to a commercial bank and borrow the money because they are not sufficiently profitable. These companies are willing to incur the higher cost of equity capital and need to share the risk with a venture capital fund. We use the term "private equity" fund primarily to refer to equity funds that are investing in companies that have grown beyond the venture stage. Most of these funds are focused on investing in leveraged change of control transactions and are also referred to as LBO, or leveraged buy-out, funds. There are also a limited number of private equity funds which will invest in non-leveraged and non-change of control transactions but, again, they are interested in relatively well established companies.

Q: What about hedge funds? Are they a factor in the capital raising process that we are discussing here?

A: Hedge funds have become a major factor in the overall capital markets, but they are not yet a big factor in the venture capital or long-term private equity markets. Hedge funds generally have a relatively short time line for holding investments, so they like to invest in companies that are, or soon will be, either public or acquired. Most venture stage investments are highly illiquid and are likely to remain so for three to five years. We are occasionally seeing a venture stage company merged into a public shell and then raising capital from hedge funds; however, liquidity is still an issue. Such complex transactions are very limited in numbers and I doubt they will reach significant volume in the near future. I have not seen a lot of hedge fund activity in the private equity market for the same reason – lack of liquidity. No doubt a large secondary market of sorts will develop for private equity or even venture capital deals but I am not yet aware of one efficient enough to attract large volumes.

Q: Let's step back and have you describe the climate for raising capital in today's market. How do you view the market?

A: If we are referring to companies that have good growth rates and have been consistently profitable, whether they want to raise growth capital, recapitalize or complete a change of control – this is an extremely good time. The private equity funds, the banks, and the mezzanine funds are all currently aggressive. There are billions of dollars that have been raised by the middle market LBO funds, and they are looking for transactions. I do not think prices being paid for well performing companies have been higher in the last 20 or 30 years. And even with some overdue credit tightening, there is still plenty of leverage available to middle market transactions. These smaller transactions never had access to the higher flying public debt markets in the first place. For them, very little has changed. The venture capital market is also quite favorable, but not as aggressive as private equity. Venture capital valuations have improved since the bursting of the tech bubble, but not as much as in the LBO market. Although there is still plenty of capital for good venture stage companies, the bursting of the tech bubble destroyed total returns for lots of venture capital funds so this sector has not been able to raise enough capital to set off another competitive streak. LBO transaction volume has increased tenfold since 2001 and venture capital transaction volume is at about the same level as it was then.

Q: There is a tagline on your website that describes your firm as "Investment Bankers to the Southeast." How has that geographic focus served your firm?

A: Ed Croft and I formed the firm with the concept that the larger full service investment banks had become focused nationally along industry verticals and on companies with large, liquid market capitalizations. We observed that this left smaller growth companies without access to really experienced advisors. There was a bit of a vacuum. We grew up serving growth companies in the Southeast. Our then current employer had recently been sold to a large Wall Street firm. It was time to make a move. Being in Atlanta, which is one of the most robust business communities anywhere in the world, has served us well. We are part of the community, which I think represents a competitive advantage. When people understand that we are part of this community and that our reputation, personally and professionally, is behind every transaction, it makes a difference. We are not here from New York or Menlo Park just for this deal. We are in Atlanta and the Southeast for our career, and each client's opinion about our performance is going to impact our reputation locally which in turn is critical to our continued success. I think that is very important in something like investment banking where business owners or managers may not be familiar with the role of investment bankers or how to differentiate between firms.

Q: So, from a geographic perspective, do you think areas outside of Silicon Valley and the Northeast have been underserved in the capital raising process?

A: Relatively speaking, yes. There is no question that most of the U.S. based institutional equity capital is domiciled in the Northeast and California. A large part of the services that we bring to entrepreneurs is our knowledge of this national marketplace. We take a company from the Southeast and help them raise capital from strategically focused funds that are based all over the country. We are bringing money to the Southeast as fast as we can. The Southeast has always been relatively undercapitalized. Changing that is a gradual ongoing process. We may never catch up but the more important point is to try to accelerate our region's positive momentum. As the Southeast continues to have success stories and to build the infrastructure necessary to attract and retain great companies, institutions will be more and more willing to allocate money to Southeast-based funds and companies. For example, Atlanta and the Research Triangle Park in North Carolina are recognized as thriving hotbeds for new innovative companies.

Q: From a capital raising process standpoint, would a company in Charlotte face a different path for funding than a company in Sunnyvale, CA, assuming the underlying idea and business model were similar?

A: If it is a venture stage company, yes it would be easier, possibly much easier, to raise the money for the California-based entity. If you are from Sunnyvale, you could visit 20 funds that may have an interest in your company within a two hour's drive. If you are in Charlotte, there may just be just one fund there that would have deep knowledge of your space, and maybe three to five in the region. But there would be twenty or thirty spread throughout the Midwest and Eastern U.S. So, although not easily quantifiable, the Charlotte company is at a disadvantage. But again, our role is to minimize or eliminate that disadvantage by making sure good companies have full national exposure to appropriate capital sources. If the Charlotte based company is a well established company with greater than $10 million to $20 million of EBITDA, it would be at no disadvantage to the California company. In fact, it may even have a slight advantage.

Q: After the Internet bubble, have you seen a shift in the ability for idea companies or true start-ups to get funding? Has venture capital completely moved upstream to companies with revenue and market traction?

A: For the most part there is no meaningful institutional capital available for companies that are only at the idea stage. There are angel groups and individuals, but not institutions. No matter how good the idea might be, the venture community wants to see a proven business model which, at minimum, means one with customers. To be fair, I would not say there are zero funds interested in this category but it is definitely a needle in a haystack. Medical devices and pharmaceuticals are an exception due to the FDA approval process and definable nature of the potential market for such products.

Q: How much revenue are we talking about? What would a typical venture stage company look like that you would be comfortable presenting to a venture fund?

A: Typically, such a company would need to have a minimum of $3 million to $10 million of revenue. Such a company may or may not be profitable, but would have identified and proven a market niche, their growth potential would be significant and they would need capital to meet the demand for their products or services. That is the ideal candidate.

Q: Are there particular industry segments where you think you are more likely to find candidates that fit that profile?

A: There is opportunity in every industry. I don't see any segments that are absolutely on fire, but Internet marketing is pretty hot. The Internet is, I think, still in the backwoods trails days. We've only begun to see what we can do with it. Business services and outsourcing are trends which appear likely to continue, enhanced by the ability to provide services remotely via the Internet. Software is increasingly important to everything we do so there are lots of opportunities in that sector. There are always opportunities in healthcare IT; businesses that are helping to speed up the process of treating patients, handling information, lowering costs and improving patient outcomes. Life sciences is another very interesting sector. Although these companies often do not fit the ideal profile described above, I personally think life sciences and alternative energy are the sectors which will present the biggest opportunities in this century. They are also the most technical and seem to present the highest risk.

Q: When you are looking at potential opportunities, what characteristics do you place the most emphasis on during the evaluation process?

A: It would be pretty much the same things anyone else would say: a proven business model and a proven management team. It is all about having a large market opportunity, reasonable barriers to entry and a management team capable of executing the business plan. Of these factors management is the most critical. Executing a business plan is a slippery ordeal. The obstacles, and even the opportunities, are always changing. New competitors surface, customers defect, capital markets contract, possibly violently. Investors are looking for managers who can adapt quickly and continually advance the ball, no matter what.

Q: Are entrepreneurs today more savvy about the capital raising process than they were 8 to 10 years ago?

A: Oh, yes. No question about it. However, if they have not been through it, they cannot really understand what the process involves; how complex raising capital has become. They often think that one investor is as good as another and that if they get a deal done, it is a good deal. If they have done a few deals they tend to assume they have seen it all. We estimate that the process we execute requires at least 1,500 hours of our time. It requires an enormous amount of specialized expertise that we continually build on, one deal at a time. Selling a company or raising capital is not about being introduced to a few funds. The optimal outcome requires a huge sales effort by someone who is well prepared and respected in the financial community. It is a very complex and time consuming process which is best accomplished by a very experienced and well organized team. Everything needs to be perfect and the process must be carefully orchestrated to create competition among investors or buyers. You can not do that while running a company.

Q: Although your firm is primarily an investment bank, you also have your own investment fund. Would you please describe the purpose behind your fund?

A: Our fund is a vehicle to enhance our capital raising transactions. It does not come into play when we are selling a company. Primarily our fund provides the opportunity to capitalize on the quality and quantity of our capital raising transaction deal flow. Secondarily, we reasoned that we should not raise money for a company unless we were willing to invest our own capital in the transaction. Our commitment gives the deal added credibility in the marketplace. For us, the capital raising process provides a unique perspective from which to make an investment decision. In a capital raising transaction, we and management typically meet with ten to fifteen selected funds having a high level of expertise in the company's business. We get to see what they all think about the company as we manage the process. In addition, being able to think like both an agent and a principal makes us better advisors.

Q: Is it unusual for an investment banking firm to also have its own venture fund to tag along on deals?

A: It is somewhat unusual, but not unique. We manage it so as to be a complement to the transaction – not a conflict. Clients and investors both like it. We usually do not take a board seat, we invest less than 10 percent of the total so we do not price the transaction or lead the syndicate. We are very comfortable paying market prices. At the end of the process it is the client's call. The key is that we have a highly efficient and unique perspective from which to make an investment decision and it adds credibility to the deal in the marketplace. Everyone benefits.

Q: What is your investment time horizon?

A: Usually three to six years. The average fund's active investment period is five years, so you are always trying to balance the remaining life of the fund with the stage of development of the investments. The average holding period has increased considerably since the 90's.

Q: Do you see a time when the IPO market will open back up again as viable exit strategy for these companies, or is it your expectation that acquisition will be the exit for the foreseeable future?

A: The IPO market has always been a window for a very small percentage of successful companies. No one should ever count on it. When a management team says their exit plan is an IPO, they mark themselves as amateurs. There are a lot of exciting things happening with venture-backed companies, but rarely does one come along that is capable of breaking out to $100 million or $200 million in revenue on their own during the typical fund's holding period. Most of them will need to be either acquired by another company or recapitalized in order to provide investors liquidity. However, one can still make 4 and 5 times his money with a successful sale of a company in 3 to 6 years. That generates a 30-50 percent IRR [internal rate of return]. That, in my opinion, is getting the job done.

Q: In closing, is there a common piece of advice that you give the entrepreneurs you work with?

A: The answer to that question could be very lengthy. There is no one suggestion, but I can offer a few thoughts. First, before embarking on a major transaction, go sit down with a couple of investment bankers. You do not have to hire one. Do not first go out and try to sell your company or securities to all known potentially interested parties as your banker may not then be able to correct the misconceptions you may have created in the marketplace by going to market prematurely. Second, when selling your company, and particularly when raising capital, meet with as many qualified interested buyers or investors as as many qualified interested buyers or investors as possible. The marketing process offers a unique opportunity to get feedback from a large number of really smart, well connected people who otherwise would not be available to you. And finally, a properly executed process will result in the best possible valuation and terms. Unless your company is large, well established and has a consistent profitable track record, no other valuation methodology is reliable.

CHAPTER 9

Darrell Glasco,
Venture Capital Relationship Manager/Southeast,
SVB Silicon Valley Bank

Glasco joined Silicon Valley Bank, a subsidiary of Silicon Valley Bancshares, in 2000 as the Venture Capital Relationship Manager for the Southeast Division. His primary role is to establish banking relationships with Venture Capital, Private Equity and Fund of Funds in the Southeast. In addition, he provides assistance to the Bank's technology clients and prospects with the appropriate introduction to Venture Capital funds within the region. Prior to joining Silicon Valley Bank, Glasco was the Vice President of Economic Development for the Metro Atlanta Chamber of Commerce where he developed relationships with venture capital firms to encourage investment in technology companies and to enhance their growth in the Atlanta area. Before moving to Atlanta, Glasco served as Vice President of Economic Development for the Greater Austin Chamber of Commerce. He has served as a judge for the Ernst & Young Entrepreneur of the Year Award and is a former member of the Texas Economic Development Council. Glasco earned a bachelor's degree in Architecture from Texas Tech University and a master's degree in Community and Regional Planning from the University of Texas in Austin.

Q: Would you please describe SVB Silicon Valley Bank and give a brief overview of the services your firm provides?

A: The company was started in 1983, and, as you can guess, in Silicon Valley. We focus on serving technology companies, life science companies, private equity funds and the premium wine market. We provide all of the same banking services that any other commercial bank would provide. Anything from dealing with foreign exchange to accounts receivable lines. We offer lines of credit and the same deposit instruments and investment instruments that any bank would offer. The significant difference with us is we don't bank the person off the street – the consumer – like a Washington Mutual would. What sets us apart from other commercial banks is our niche focus, deep industry knowledge, and extensive network of relationships in the business sectors I just mentioned.

Q: As the name would indicate, and with headquarters in Santa Clara, your firm has strong ties to Silicon Valley, but you have offices around the country, including where you are based in Atlanta. Would you explain your geographic strategy?

A: Through our parent company, SVB Financial Group, we have 27 U.S. offices in every major technology center. We have a presence everywhere that there is a concentration of companies in the markets we serve. Our structure may vary based on the market that we are in. We don't dictate structure on the market; the market dictates its structure on us. For example, on the West Coast, we have teams that may specialize in semiconductors and biotechnology, because there is a critical mass of those kinds of companies, whereas on the East Coast, especially in the Southeast, we have teams that specialize in software companies. We also have three international offices, in India, China, and the U.K., which are focused on allowing our clients to take advantage of cross-border opportunities with those markets.

Q: How does SVB Silicon Valley Bank approach acquiring its clients?

A: While we use marketing and advertising as a branding tool, those are not our tools of choice for new client generation. We attract our clients through our network. A big part of that network is the venture firms, or funds we've had relationships with since our inception in 1983. Through these firms, we've established longstanding relationships with serial entrepreneurs. A significant amount of our business comes from these serial entrepreneurs, who have worked with us before. You'll see the CEO or CFO of a company that's with us through his or her third or fourth company. Most of our clients come through referrals because of the unique nature of our business. Our clients range from emerging companies, to growth companies, to established companies as well as private equity firms. We provide innovative credit solutions that other banks will not provide. Let's say you're a company that's just beginning to ramp up and you expect a lot of revenue a year from now. We can help bridge that gap in current cash needs until the revenue starts to arrive. We understand these kinds of business models. In fact, we were one of the very first banks to look at ways to serve companies that had no revenue at all. We are comfortable in those situations because of our relationships with the venture investors who are funding these companies. We don't panic when a company isn't on plan. We've actually picked up clients dropped by other banks when they failed to meet certain projections. They may have a hiccup financially but are still a good, fundamental opportunity. But a lot of banks can't get beyond the structure of traditional business and are not looking at the bigger picture. That's really where we excel.

Q: What are some of the typical characteristics of companies that are your clients?

A: The majority of our clients range from no revenue to about $200 million in revenue, although we have a growing number of larger clients up to $1 billion in revenue. They are all growing companies. For the most part, our clients are technology-based and have intellectual property behind that technology, which they own or are in the process of owning. And the vast majority of them are venture backed.

Q: If your companies are all growing and most have been successful in raising outside capital, what is the motivation for taking on bank debt?

A: Well there is always a trade-off between debt and equity. As these companies take on more equity-based funding, the founders and initial backers lose more of their interest in the company. So with each new round of funding, the ownership is further diluted. That's not necessarily a bad thing, because it may be better to own 10 percent of a billion dollar company than 100 percent a $100 million company. But there has to be a balance between how much equity is given up and when that equity is given up. That's the reason a lot of funds like to bring in debt, and a lot of management teams like to bring in debt. It helps the management team retain more ownership of the company while giving them the operating capital to increase its value.

Q: From an entrepreneur's perspective, is it appropriate to look at bringing on debt very early in a company's development as opposed to going out and getting friends and family or angel capital?

A: Every situation is different and I'm not suggesting that debt is a replacement for equity funding. The two can work together to help a business achieve its growth objectives. But taking a step back, I think it's important that before entrepreneurs even think about bringing in an investor, or taking on debt, they first ought to develop a banking relationship. The business has to run a deposit account somewhere and it's good to use a relationship with a banker as a starting point before the need for funding is critical. That's the best time to develop that relationship because the entrepreneur will have a better understanding of how the bank operates, and the bank will have some exposure to how the entrepreneur manages his or her affairs. If the bank is given the opportunity to understand what your business is all about, there is a better chance of developing a relationship that can be productive, especially if things don't go as planned.

Q: How would you describe your role at SVB Silicon Valley Bank? Do you interact with companies and entrepreneurs, or are you strictly on the relationship side with the VCs?

A: Actually, I do both, but my job is banking VCs. I have about 40 venture funds that are my clients and through them I get involved with companies. As the funds I work with are looking for companies to invest in, I see the finances and I see what investments they are making and how they are structured. I work with my colleagues who see a lot of companies and help introduce those companies to the funds I work with. So it's through those introductions that I get involved with the companies and I deal with them at a fairly high level, but I work closely with the funds on a much deeper level.

Q: Are the 40 funds that are part of your client portfolio all Southeastern based?

A: Yes, for the most part, but it extends up to Baltimore.

Q: How do you view the venture capital business in the Southeast?

A: I've had the debate with a number of people who want us to believe there is a dearth of capital in the Southeast, but from my perspective, it's just not true. I've never seen a good idea fail to get funding. The issue isn't finding capital; it's finding a good company to put the capital in. I think the people who make that argument are focusing on the wrong thing. They are focusing on the effect and not the cause. The community has to support entrepreneurs and encourage risk-taking and the capital will follow. The Advanced Technology Development Center (ATDC) at Georgia Tech has been phenomenal. There should be more efforts like that to support entrepreneurs. Could the region benefit from having more local funds? Probably, but in the meantime you have capital coming into the region from funds based elsewhere. You would be surprised at how often the funds are in here from the West Coast and Boston. As I said, if the idea is good and the management team is solid, it will get funded.

Q: Is there a downside to capital coming into a region from the outside?

A: There are times when those funds don't have loyalty to the region. For example, there was an ATDC company that got funding from a West Coast VC, but one of the conditions of the investment was that the firm had to relocate to California. In this case, the entrepreneur weighed the options and decided it was in the best interest of the company to pick up and move. I suppose if there were more local funds available, more funds from outside the region would be interested in having local co-investors to help them keep an eye on their investments.

Q: Let's approach the question from a slightly different perspective. Does an entrepreneur have more difficulty raising capital when he doesn't have a Silicon Valley address?

A: No. As I said, good companies get funded. Maybe in the past geography played a greater role in the process, but now funds will go to the deal. If an entrepreneur has talked to multiple VCs and can't raise funds, the entrepreneur then has to start questioning the business plan. There is so much capital looking for good deals that several passes would indicate a fundamental problem with the business model. Perhaps the market isn't big enough; perhaps the competition is too great. Maybe the VCs don't believe the team can deliver the product. There are many reasons why a company won't get funded, but its address isn't likely to be on the list.

Q: In your experience, is there a typical mistake you see companies make when they approach the venture community for funding?

A: I think the typical mistake entrepreneurs make is that they don't give a quick summary of the idea. They have to realize that these people are seeing hundreds of plans every week, if not every day. The presentation material has to work just like a résumé. How do you make yourself stand out? Get to the point quickly. There are three things that an entrepreneur should explain: Who the management team is and why the investor should have confidence in it. What the market opportunity is – and be realistic about it. And finally, how you are going after the market – your approach. They will appreciate those three things in a one-page document more than you know. I'm not saying that you don't need to have all of the background for a follow-up meeting, but when you consider how extremely busy they are – especially the really good funds – a one-pager makes a lot more sense as a way to get their attention.

Q: Does SVB Silicon Valley Bank itself make venture investments?

A: One of our affiliate business groups, SVB Capital, makes venture capital investments through our affiliated venture funds. SVB Capital is the private equity arm of SVB Financial Group. The funds managed by SVB Capital invest in companies directly and invest in the venture funds that, in turn, invest in companies, a "fund of funds."

Q: Not every start-up company is suited for venture capital. Is there a litmus test that an entrepreneur can apply to determine if his business is suitable for venture funding?

A: I think the biggest factor to consider is product. Have you got a product that can be sold in large numbers? In understanding the economics of funds, they are only going to put money into a business that has the potential to scale large enough to create an economic return for the fund to pay its investors. A lot of companies are better off as mom and pops. There are a lot of companies that don't want to be more than $10 million or $15 million in revenue ever, but those aren't venture opportunities. The funds are betting on big returns. So in order to be successful in raising venture capital, you have to be realistic about your chances of reaching a scale that will create those types of returns. If you have any doubts, you have to go back and analyze your business model before approaching the VCs.

Q: Let's suppose the entrepreneur has determined his business meets the scalability test. What should his next consideration be before approaching a venture fund?

A: The entrepreneur has to network and start getting to know some of the VCs. Getting venture funding is only half of the equation. The other half is that this is a relationship, like a marriage. You will be dealing with these people constantly; they will be on your board and you will be very intimate with them for a long period of time. If you don't like these people, and you take their money, you are going to have a difficult time. So getting to know which VCs you can work with is important. It doesn't mean that you necessarily have to love each other, go fishing or hang out, but there has to be a common mindset and a relationship where you can actually work together. The other thing I would seek to learn is what other value, aside from money, will the fund bring to the relationship. All funds are not created equal. There are some funds that have people who are extremely well connected in specific industries.

Q: What is the best way for entrepreneurs to approach a venture fund?

A: Companies don't do nearly enough homework in determining which funds to contact. There are the blasters who send their business plan to every VC that they get an address for. That's a really bad idea; that's the worst thing an entrepreneur could do. These blasters don't realize that these funds all know each other and they talk to each other. Entrepreneurs who research the funds that are most likely to invest in their area, do their homework on these funds, and approach them from a position of knowledge about the fund, have a much better chance of getting an audience. But I'll tell you that less than 10 percent of the companies I've encountered really follow that advice.

Q: Is it advantageous for companies to participate in group business plan presentations? Do VCs really find deals through this process?

A: There are a lot of events for companies to present to funds and I think it is debatable as to how useful those events are in raising capital. At SVB Financial Group, we've taken the opposite approach. We will bring in one fund and have it present to a dozen or so of our companies. They can explain the fund, how it operates and its investment philosophy. We keep it intimate. That allows everybody to have some interaction. With one fund presenting, the companies can ask some pretty pertinent questions. To me, it is more educational and it gives them an opportunity to do something they normally wouldn't get to do. When the companies are presenting, they are trying to convince someone to give money, to invest, whereas this way there is not a lot of pressure, the companies are not in raising mode and can ask questions in a more relaxed setting.

Q: In closing, are there any parting words of advice for the entrepreneurs reading this interview?

A: Do the homework we discussed and build a good company. I'll stand by this: if you've got a company that is doing well – and by doing well I mean generating revenue to the point that it looks like there is a market for the product – you are going to get funded. The VCs don't see enough good companies, so shortage of capital is not the issue. I can tell you unequivocally – and I would bet my salary for the year – that if you present me with a good company with solid fundamentals, I'll get it funded even if it's in one of the most unheard of places in Georgia. I can get any good company funded, because that's how much capital is out there.

CHAPTER 10

Alan Koenning, Fund Manager
UPS Strategic Enterprise Fund

Koenning is the Fund Manager for the UPS Strategic Enterprise Fund, which is the private equity strategic investment arm of UPS. The Fund is a corporate venture capital group which focuses on developing critical partnerships and acquiring knowledge returns from its investments in information technology companies and emerging market-spaces. Koenning's responsibilities include working with various UPS departments and business units in identifying areas of strategic interest, researching potential investments, negotiating agreements and acting as a corporate liaison with Fund companies. Koenning has been with UPS for 16 years, including assignments in Corporate UPS, UPS e-Ventures, and UPS Supply Chain Solutions. He graduated from Duke University and has an MBA from the University of Georgia.

Q: To lay a foundation for this discussion, would you give your thoughts on the role that corporate venture plays in the capital raising process?

A: There are a variety of roles that corporate venture can play in the capital raising process depending upon the target of a particular corporation. Within corporate venture capital, different corporations have different goals and motivations in terms of what they want to achieve. Some are looking to close a knowledge gap; some are looking to develop business relationships and partnerships where they can leverage their key capabilities in bringing new products to market. Some are looking for potential acquisition targets and they want to be involved with a company beforehand. At UPS, our investments are about learning and understanding whether a technology is going to be adopted in the marketplace. Our focus is more strategic; it is about keeping our eyes and ears closest to technology development.

Q: Many corporations, including UPS, launched their funds before or during the Internet bubble in the late 1990's. After the Internet bubble, the majority of these companies withdrew from the venture market, but UPS has stuck with it through the years. What were the factors that led to your decision to remain active?

A: The fact that our fund is focused on early stage technology investments primarily with the goal of understanding technology has been the key factor in keeping us active. Many of the companies who started corporate venture capital groups during the dot com days, jumped in for purely financial motivations and not with a strategic purpose as we had established with our fund. Our fund focuses on those early stage companies with technologies that might impact how we operate or how our customers conduct business, so there is a strategic relevance to us. Whether or not a company we invest in proves to be financially successful or not, we are still learning something that is bringing an understanding about the market place into our organization. The value of that goes beyond simply evaluating an investment strategy based on financial returns.

Q: With the financial markets improved, are you seeing more corporations getting involved? Is there a corporate return to venture investing?

A: Yes. We are seeing more corporations who recognize the strategic value of being an early stage investor. They've moved from purely a financial motivation to more of a strategic focus. None of us want to be in this to just throw away money. Clearly, financial rigor is a critical component of the investment process, but the financial rewards are not the sole motivation for corporations doing corporate venture investing.

Q: Specific to UPS, what is the investment philosophy that drives your investment strategy?

A: The UPS Strategic Enterprise Fund falls within our corporate strategy group. This group is tasked with establishing a longer term vision for the organization. Part of that lies in identifying trends that might impact the organization. Ultimately, the Strategic Enterprise Fund becomes a bridge for the company. We find emerging companies doing work within some of those trends, establish ties with them and perhaps invest. In this way, our business functions can get closer relationships to those trends and help in understanding how those trends can impact, or potentially impact, their business unit. The Strategic Enterprise Fund creates a more concrete relationship between things that might impact our organization in the future – say in a two- to five-year timeframe – and bring them a little closer to the business units. Our investments in technology companies allow our business units to be closer to these things, but without becoming distracted or having to spend a lot of time on these issues. We like to say our investments are in those things that are on the edge of the desk in most people's offices. They are investments in ideas and technologies our frontline people know they should be thinking about, but may not have the time to spend thinking strategically about. We help them bridge this gap. We bring this together by allowing them to provide open input and we share with them the learning we gain from these investments.

Q: Within that framework, what kind of companies have you invested in?

A: We have invested in 32 companies, all driven off the fact that we are looking for companies that potentially impact how we operate or how our customers conduct business. Many of the companies that are interesting to us are logistics related. More recently, some of our investments have been in RFID [radio frequency identification] technologies. Some of our investments have been in other technologies that could potentially impact how our people conduct their jobs. For example, we have been investing in a myriad of thin panel displays and electronic components that go into mechanisms and devices that our operations groups may use. We have also been making investments in information technology associated with real time data management and event management. We're a $47.5 billion company and there are lots of things that impact how we operate. And we have a broad customer base, so we are looking for things that we'd like to understand more about and we invest in those where we find the greatest strategic value.

Q: Even though strategic value is the key component of your investment philosophy, would please elaborate further about the financial consideration of your investments?

A: Our primary focus is the strategic knowledge that we can gain. If a direct financial benefit comes out of it, that's all for the best. We are not evaluating any investments purely on the financial merits of a deal. Clearly, as I said before, we don't want to make investments that are financially imprudent, but venture fund type returns are not our motivation. With that said, however, we are focused on business models and trying to understand whether they are going to be successful. We look at expenses and how the business is using their cash and how our investment would be deployed. We fall into the category of an early stage investor versus some of the other investors who would be later stage when the business has traction in the marketplace.

Q: As an early stage investor, what size investments do you make and how much equity in the firm would that investment typically represent?

A: Our investments have been anywhere from $100,000 to $1 million with our typical investment in the $250,000 to $500,000 range. We are usually an A or B round investor where valuations can range anywhere from $3 million to $12 million. So, you can see we are not taking a big chunk of the company. We are not there to be a controlling interest.

Q: Does UPS prefer to go it alone with its investments or does the fund co-invest with other funds?

A: We are strictly a co-investment fund. We are relying on other venture folks who are better trained and have the experience in managing early stage technology start ups than we are to take the lead. We certainly interact with the firms who approach us, and if we like them, we will present them or introduce them to other investors and work with them in their development process for funding.

Q: Do you find yourself being sought out by the traditional venture funds as a co-investor, or do you primarily bring deals to those firms?

A: It's multifaceted in terms of the deals we've done. We are approached by VCs for potential deals that they think would be of interest to us and so our relationships with VCs are very important to us. Our name brand brings potential entrepreneurs to us directly as well, and, therefore, we make introductions to other VCs that we think would have a relevant interest in a particular technology. After the Internet bubble, we had a dry spell for a while when there wasn't a lot going on, so we didn't have as much interaction with the venture community. With the activity returning, we've had to re-engage. Following a co-investor model means that it's important being top of mind with VCs when they are reaching out to do a deal. We spend a lot of time being out in the market and interacting with them in their geographies, just talking about their deal flow and comparing notes about companies and deals that we recently made.

Q: How many potential deals do you investigate in a year?

A: We probably see 500 or 600 companies a year in varying degrees. We quickly make an assessment as to whether there's an interest from a strategic standpoint. Then we go to the particular business unit or functional area that we think would be most interested in learning about a particular company and ask them whether the idea is something they would like to evaluate short-term from a potential vendor standpoint. If they come back and say "This is interesting, but it's a little too far out for us right now, we don't have an immediate need," then we ask them if it represents something that could potentially impact them in the future. Based on that response, we'll evaluate it from an investment standpoint.

Q: What is your approval process? Do your investments go through a committee? Do they go all the way to the CEO of the company? In other words, where is the sign-off?

A: Our model is very dependent on finding internal sponsors within a business unit or functional area. We do our diligence in coordination with the sponsor and ultimately gain their agreement that an opportunity is something they believe is worthy of an investment. Then we put together an investment proposal that we submit to our investment committee for review. The committee is a cross section of strategy people, IT people and Senior VP's. By the time it gets to the investment committee, it should be a pretty solid deal. During the committee review, they may ask us additional questions, but we try to give them a pretty tight definition of what the investment is and what the learning opportunity is for the business unit.

Q: UPS is headquartered in Atlanta, but you have a giant global business operation. Do you have any geographic focus with the investments you make?

A: Our current focus is the U.S., and that's really driven off the fact that we haven't found enough deal flow in other parts of the world to justify getting involved in non-US geographies, although we keep our eyes open to some technology companies out of Israel, and we are starting to keep our eyes open to some opportunities in Asia. One of our portfolio companies is now a European company, but that was the result of an acquisition. We do keep our eyes on geographies outside of the U.S. to make sure that we understand what is occurring there from an investment standpoint as well. We have no boundaries in terms of geographies within the U.S. currently.

Q: As you observe the market in the U.S., do you find any geographic differences in the capital raising process?

A: Yes, without a doubt. We find differences in terms of VCs; we find a difference in the entrepreneurial skill set and motivations; we find a difference in the technologies and various types of companies that spring up. Some portions of the U.S. have much better ecosystems than others to support venture related start-up companies. The two strongest areas clearly are Boston and Silicon Valley where there is a very well established ecosystem for startups to flourish. On the West Coast, particularly in the Palo Alto area, we see that information technology is one of the core area strengths. And a lot of what would be called Web 2.0 – user generated solutions – are coming from there. In Boston, we see financial related software as a strength. A lot of industrial types of solutions come from both of those geographies. The VCs have been established and have been around a while, and there is a huge number of VCs in both of those geographies. We are less likely to do a deal on the West Coast because in most cases, the VCs are pretty independent and have experience and are pretty confident about their investments. We are invited into more deals in the Northwest and in Texas. Those are much more collegial types of environment where VC's try to syndicate deals vs. doing deals alone. In the Southeast, you just don't have the number of VCs now to create an ecosystem. Also, the number of entrepreneurs available to start companies is important to establishing that ecosystem. The number of people who have the background and experience and are willing to take the risk are clearly greater in Boston and on the West Coast. Now we are starting to see more of that occur within Seattle too, but there are not as many entrepreneurs in the Atlanta area willing to step out to create companies.

Q: With those ecosystems – as you call them – established in Silicon Valley and Boston is it easier for a start-up to get funding there?

A: I don't know if I'd say it's easier, but funds are more available. The VCs are still very selective in who gets the money.

Q: Are there advantages to receiving funding from a corporation such as yours. For example, would an investment from UPS come with a business deal that provides revenue?

A: First, it's important to note that we will not invest in a company that we already have a business relationship with. With our investment focus on strategic learning, an existing business relationship with somebody would already give us a close enough tie to them and we would not make an investment on top of that. Now, if a business relationship develops after we've made the investment, that's fine. Given that we try to have strategic alignment, it would be natural for opportunities to develop and that has occurred in the past. We also think there are other advantages from our investment. We bring subject matter expertise, we bring industry perspective, and it is a perspective from a company who has probably done a sizeable amount of research and has customer interaction and an understanding of the marketplace. We can introduce the company to experts and bring them relationships. They can use us as a sounding board when developing their business model and ultimately determining how to best run their company. One of the things we've heard from VCs is that they have a challenge getting potential customers' perspective. We bring that to the table and answer the tough questions that the VCs know to ask. Sometimes the entrepreneurs aren't overly willing to listen to the VCs, but when you hear from a real potential customer like us it's a little more direct and impactful.

Q: What management role does UPS play in its portfolio companies? Do you require a board seat or do you have some other type of advisory role?

A: We ask for board observation rights for all of our investments. We bring in somebody from a business unit or function to act as a board observer. We are bringing somebody who has the most relevant subject matter expertise and knowledge to the table. They participate in the board meetings and we train them not to tell our companies what to do, but to ask key questions and to share their views about the marketplace, but the role is not to tell the company what they should or shouldn't be doing.

Q: Drawing on your experience of looking at 500 to 600 companies a year, what would your advice be for the entrepreneur hoping to raise capital from your fund?

A: They must understand what we do. We are an early stage investor, but we are not investing in things that are just ideas. There has to be some traction associated with it. It doesn't necessarily mean you have to have a customer, although that would be nice. We are not an angel investor, we are later stage than that and expect the entrepreneur to demonstrate that he's got something that has a high probability of working in the marketplace. Another of our criteria for an investment is that a management team has been formed and there is a vision as to where they want to take the business. They must demonstrate a pretty good understanding as to how they are going to use this money – what it is going to be used for and what the results are going to be from the use of the money.

CHAPTER 11

Rick Winston, President
E.H. Winston and Associates

Winston founded E.H. Winston & Associates, a management consulting practice, in 1985 and currently specializes in the areas of operational and financial restructuring, strategic validation and profitable business growth. Winston is chairman, President and CEO of Inisoft Corporation, an online software development company, and is on the board of directors of Dynamic Leisure Corp. From 1997 through 1998, he was President and Chief Executive Officer of Microforum, Inc., an online enterprise solutions developer. From 1994 through 1996, Winston was President and Chief Operating Officer of Sound Source Interactive, Inc., an interactive CD-Rom publisher of entertainment content. He was President and Chief Executive Officer of Computer Data Information Systems, Inc., an enterprise software developer, from 1985 to 1991. Winston holds a BBA from Memphis State University.

Q: Considering all that raising capital entails, do you think we are in a favorable time for entrepreneurs?

A: My personal view is that I am seeing a lot of money out there. There is a tremendous amount of money that is available. But I am seeing many capital organizations moving up stream. They are looking for larger transactions. They don't want to have as many small transactions in their portfolio as they may have had in the past, and that eliminates the availability of money for smaller organizations. There is money out there; it's just that I am finding the low end market, or what I call the emerging growth market, and the lower end of the middle market as having a more difficult time identifying investment capital. Bottom line; I truly believe that this segment of the market has become under served as capital groups continue to move up stream and are only looking at larger transactions.

Q: When embarking on the process of raising capital, entrepreneurs tend to look toward angel investors and venture capital firms, but you don't see that as the complete landscape. When it comes to raising capital what are you seeing as the primary alternatives?

A: I'm finding that the hedge funds are still investing an unbelievable amount of money. And, yes, they will invest in private companies. Although private entitles don't provide the liquidity for these groups to get out if they are not happy with the performance of the company, there is still money available. The hedge funds are investing both debt capital and convertible debt capital. It seems to be the convertible debt transactions have been and still continue to be – how do we say "the flavor of the month" or the transaction of preference; this gives the fund an opportunity to enjoy a monthly or quarterly coupon on the money that they've invested and at the same time, if the company takes off, they can convert their debt to equity and take a real piece of the upside. So, personally I see more of the hedge fund market as an alternative source of funding for micro cap or small emerging growth private entities.

Q: Are there other alternatives that you are seeing emerging; other types of private equity institutions involved in this?

A: Yes. There are private equity groups that will look at smaller companies with revenues of $10 million or more. But these deals are usually part of a larger transaction. Typically, that $10 million size company would be too small for the larger private equity groups, but as a bolt on – or a clamp on as we call it – to a larger investment, then all the rules go off the table and they will take a look at it.

Q: You've used the phrases hedge funds and private equity. Would those be the typical way these types of institutions are described, or are there some other descriptions that would be appropriate for our readers to understand?

A: I think the terms "hedge fund" and "private equity" seems to be the naming convention that everybody understands. They seem to have more money today than other groups. I am finding that many individuals in venture capital have started to refer to themselves over the last few years as private equity. It seems like they wanted to move away for whatever reason from the naming convention of venture capitalist, but also I think they did that because they are moving upstream with the size of their investments. I think to find a fund today that will take an idea and invest in it, is rare. I personally don't work in that circle and don't know any players like that anymore. However, I am finding investors who are looking for a company that has some traction; a company that has some history of recognizing revenue. They want companies that have customers because, of course, when you have customers, every time your customer buys, it is a validation that you have something of value to offer. So in getting back to the premise of the question, private equity groups and hedge funds are well recognized throughout this country.

Q: Having said that they are well known throughout the country; does that translate into activity across the country? Are these types of deals getting done only in California or

the Northeast, or do you see hedge funds and private equity companies doing these kinds of investments in other areas as well?

A: Oh, they are all over the country. I would say the largest concentration, of course, is in New York City. That is still the financial capital of the world. I know of more hedge funds in New York than I know in other one geographic location, but there are hedge funds and private equity groups all over the U.S. The interesting part about it is the ones that are out of New York seem to be more regionally inclined to make their investments. They like to have investments within a day's travel distance. They don't want to have to travel too far to check on their investments.

Q: The type of companies we've talked about for these alternative type transactions are companies that have begun to attract customers, generate revenue and are further up the food chain. Is that an accurate description?

A: I think it is. I don't personally get involved in a pre-revenue or start-up organization. I found over the years that it's a little too difficult for my taste to work with a company that doesn't have all the attributes in place that I would recognize as a viable business opportunity. Most of the groups that I would be looking to for alternative financing are going to be looking for period over period revenue growth and some form of traction. They are going to be looking for a company that is growing; that has a great opportunity for growth in the next one to three years.

Q: What about industry segments? Are the types of deals that you are discussing here more suited to a particular industry sector such as technology or healthcare? Or do you find these types of deals being done across the board?

A: Deals are being done across the board, but there are a lot of these funds that will not dabble in technology. We still have people who remember the bubble bursting and taking out companies that had been funded when they didn't have the basic attributes of a real business. As far as industry segments are concerned, healthcare is big. Brick and mortar businesses, especially manufacturing, are never going to go out of style. Some groups still love technology, but some funds will tell you: "We don't understand cutting edge technology, and we don't want our investment dependent on whether this technology gets completed or not."

Q: In your role of assisting in the capital raising process, what do you look for in a company?

A: There are two basic questions we consider when looking at a company to take out for investment. Do we have a real good story that will get the attention of the investment fund? And can we package that story around the facts of how we will repay the debt – if it's a debt instrument deal – or what the upside is, if it's an equity deal? What it comes down to is the businesses' ability to tell a good story that makes me comfortable.

Q: In your view of this process, how important is the management team? In other words is management more important to you than the underlying business model?

A: Management is still the number one asset. No fund will put money behind someone they're not comfortable with. And, I say that as someone who has worked in the restructuring world where we replace management all the time. In a growth company, management is critical. It's one of the six attributes that I look for anytime I go into a business. But it's not just management; it is also the people within the organization. A growth company cannot be totally on the shoulders of just one individual, but that company will not grow without a driving force. You need to have someone who is committed to the task of making the company grow. Yes, I guess you would say management is critical, absolutely critical.

Q: You said that management is one of six attributes that you use in evaluating potential deals, could you tell our readers about the other five attributes?

A: Absolutely. And by the way this goes across all product lines and all industries. The first attribute I look for is margin. If the company doesn't have ample margin then all we are really doing is exchanging dollars between the company's customers and their creditors. If there isn't proper or adequate margin, then this is a total waste of time. The second attribute is distribution. Many great products never got out of the garage because management couldn't set up distribution. They didn't know how to get their product or products out to the market to their targeted customers. So without distribution, you can die of loneliness. Before, we were talking about people wherein people are the third attribute. People – including management – are critically important. The forth attribute I look for is technology. To get financed today, you've got to have basic back office systems in place. Bigger companies respect the fact that small companies are a lot more agile than they are, but the bigger companies don't like to do business with smaller companies unless the back office technology is in place. Bigger companies are scared that they will get embarrassed in public if a small company they're doing business with "stumbles." So, having technology in place as part of your product offering or simply as the back office to your business is critical. The fifth attribute is customers. Every time a customer buys something – whether it is a product or a service – this is a validation that you have something of value. Something of value that people are willing to pay for. You just can't ignore this attribute when evaluating a business. The last attribute we look for is cash flow. But out of these six attributes, cash flow is usually the one thing missing. At the same time, if you have margin and distribution, you can rebuild cash flow. So again the six attributes I look for in evaluating any business would be margin, distribution, people, technology, customers and cash flow.

Q: That's a very succinct way for our readers to see how people who are providing capital evaluate a business. Could you take it one step further describe how a typical deal you are involved in might be structured?

A: When I get brought in on a transaction, the underlying rule is very simple: Management runs the company and I run the transaction. If you are trying to complete a transaction, and the company's business takes a turn for the worse, you've just crippled the transaction. Running a business is a full time job, which leaves little room for managing investment transactions. Growing a business takes time and a half; that's why many successful CEOs and presidents put in those long 10, 12, 14 hour days if not longer because that's is what is required to grow a business. So, needless to say, if a president, CEO or entrepreneur goes out and tries to raise the capital himself, he's taking time away from either running or growing his business; bottom line: something has to suffer. So when I come in on a transaction, and I am introduced to the members of the board and to the management group, it is understood up front: You run the company and I run the transaction. From there, we will sit down together and package the story. You can't sit there and just assume that an investor group will understand the business. You have to appreciate that this transaction is in competition with hundreds, if not thousands of other transactions that are also looking for capital. We are all fighting for the attention of the investment fund. Typically, the investment fund will not get as passionate about the company, as the president or the CEO is, but they have to understand it. Once the story is packaged, it has to be approved for accuracy by the management. And once that's done, then management is free to go back to running the company, and that's where my job of sourcing the market, as we call it, begins. We will try to identify sources of capital and bring together what I like to call a beauty pageant that will hopefully include 2, 3 or 4 perspective investors and lenders who like the transaction and who realize they are in a bit of a competition to make the investment. But the truth is most investments don't get funded. A lot of investments only see one perspective investor. We've been extremely fortunate in pulling together a beauty pageant for our clients. At that point, the company will have a chance to decide who they will want to partner with and whose money they want to take.

Q: In a particular deal like that, how much equity is up for grabs? Are these typically deals where a minority position

is for sale or do these type of investors look for majority control?

A: It depends on the stage of the company and most importantly, the investing criteria of the fund. If a private company has revenue and traction and can service debt, it will typically be a convertible debt type of instrument, or a debt instrument with warrants. If the company takes off, the lender or the investor has the opportunity to participate in the upside. If it's a public entity, you are going to find more investors willing to take a flyer on equity because of the perceived liquidity. At the same time, when investing in a private company, if you don't have control, you are really a captive audience. In a public entity, there is that perceived liquidity that if you don't like the way things are going, you can get out. But if there isn't adequate trading volume, liquidity is only a perception and that logic falls off the table.

Q: So private companies would be looking at perhaps having to give up control, while an existing public entity may have a little more leverage?

A: That is correct. When people invest – it's hard to get people to invest in a private entity, because there is no guaranteed or assumed exit. There is no liquidity and if things are not working out, as an investor, you are a captive audience.

Q: Is it a strategy for a private company to become a public company before trying to raise this type of capital by merging into a public shell?

A: Absolutely not. Every week I talk to private company owners and the idea of going public does come up. I try to caution them that they don't want to do that unless there is an absolute guarantee of money on the table. I would never, ever, ever suggest to any CEO of a private company, that he go public unless there is a raise of capital simultaneously with the conversion into a public entity. Now, there are people out there who would have you believe that if you're public, you have access to all sorts of new capital and there is some element of truth to that. But, the problem with being public is that your whole life, time commitments and business structure changes. Moreover, the cost of being public in this day and age is brutally expensive due in part to the Sarbanes-Oxley legislation. This legislation requires documentation for all sorts of internal processes, which is very expensive. So with all that's involved, when I'm to meet with a private entity thinking about going public, I say let's sit down and talk about this, because this is an expensive step you are getting ready to embark on. I always tell them that unless you've got a real upside to your story and your story holds together, it may not be the right decision at all.

Q: Can you provide an example of the deal that would represent a successful transaction?

A: I was working with a manufacturing group that was about 20 years old with revenue of about $25 million. Over the previous two years they had losses, not big losses, but their financial statements at the end of those years reported losses. They were trying to refinance their current debt which was with a fund that was what we call toxic. In other words, they were paying dearly at the time; they were paying prime + 4 and each member of the management team had a personal guarantee supporting the debt. They had a subordinate debt holder that hadn't been paid a penny in three years because he was totally subordinated to the senior debt. And there was only a 6-month lock up on the interest rate so every six months the fund would ratchet up the interest rate. I came in and met with the company and the CEO. Just like I said earlier it was a clear understanding up front: you run your company and I'll run the transaction. We packaged the company's story and we were fortunate enough that within six weeks we had a real beauty contest. After sourcing the market, we had three prospective lenders who had been fully disclosed on the company's past and the company's prospect for the future. All three prospective lenders wanted the business, and we got into a real competitive situation where my client was able to select one of the three perspective lenders that he preferred to work with. My client walked away with a transaction that was prime plus ¾ of a point. No personal guarantees, and instead of having a six month lock on the interest rate, it was a three year lock as long as the company didn't break it's covenants. As I explained to the CEO, if you don't screw up, you are golden.

Q: What was the compelling piece of the story that you packaged that attracted these competitive bids?

A: Since they had losses, we had to show that the company had at least turned the corner; had corrected the deficiencies in its process. They had good margin and they had good distribution. The new CEO had been brought in by the founder. The founder had been in charge from the beginning of the company and when the company started to lose money, that's when they brought in the new CEO. We packaged the story around the new management: this is what he's done; this is what he's been able to move away from and what he has been able to improve upon. We were able to say: this is what his budget and projections look like and the story just held together.

Q: Conversely, can you describe a situation where a transaction failed?

A: Typically a transaction fails when management cannot move the company forward as it has projected. We'll sit down, and we'll package the story and the projections are in line with what everyone believes can be accomplished. Then for one reason or another during the middle of a transaction, business tails off and they start moving in the wrong direction. Management needs to make some timely decisions, but probably the number one factor contributing to a failed deal that I have found over the years is that management in these situations always believes there is sunshine around the next corner. They keep holding out; they are not prepared to make changes and are not willing to make the tough, timely decisions that are required at that point in time. One thing learned from the work we do is that you must implement change daily. Most managers don't think about this; you can't afford to wait 90 days and incur losses that put you in a hole. Every single day of every week, you need to be looking at those people that are on your staff and those people that work with your company either indirectly or directly and look at their contribution. If they are not making the contribution you were expecting, you need to part ways. You need to cut expenses and be looking at how to manage expenses daily. During a capital/debt raise, I find that when companies start to track in the wrong direction, it's because management hasn't been able to control the business and wasn't willing to make some tough, timely decisions. They were not prepared to implement change to avoid the losses accumulating.

Q: When you sit down to work with a management team on a deal, what's the first piece of advice you give?

A: If we are going to work together, you are going to run the company, and I am going to run the transaction. I know I've already said this before, but it's critically important. By the way, that's not advice; it's a non-negotiable requirement of us working together. We have to have agreed to it up front. From an advice perspective, I preach that you've got to be able to tell your story concisely and get right to the point. Don't ramble, don't babble, just get right to the point. If someone asks you a question, you've got eight seconds to answer the question or they are going to believe the question caught you off guard or that maybe you don't know the answer to the question. So they must be prepared and rehearsed; wherein, all responses have to be short. The perspective investor must know he is talking to a CEO who is truly in control of his company.

CHAPTER 12

Jim Stratigos
Chief Executive Officer
Jacket Micro Devices (JMD)

Stratigos is a successful high-technology entrepreneur with executive and CEO experience in a number of startups over the past 20 years. He was founder and CEO of Media4, Inc., where he pioneered the technology to distribute Internet content over direct broadcast satellite networks. EchoStar acquired Media4 in 1999. Stratigos was also a co-founder at Tridom Corporation. Involved in wireless communications management, engineering and marketing for over 30 years, Stratigos has held senior positions at Scientific-Atlanta, Georgia Tech Research Institute and Motorola. He is a founding member of Atlanta Technology Angels. He holds BSEE and MSEE degrees from Georgia Institute of Technology.

Q: As an entrepreneur with experience in several start up businesses would you give your impression of the capital raising process?

A: In terms of what I know from having raised capital in Atlanta and what I read about the rest of the country, it's a long hard process. Unless you are in Silicon Valley and have had five successful startups – rather five startups whether they were successful or not – it will be a long and time consuming process. It can be frustrating, but it can be exciting; that's my experience at least. It never happens the way you think it will happen and it generally takes longer than you expect. The investors you thought would be very interested will turn out to not be the ones who are very interested in what you are doing. You spend a lot of time educating investors on what you do.

Q: That last comment is interesting, because venture capitalists seem to think that entrepreneurs don't do enough homework when approaching them for funding. What did you mean?

A: Well, it's a shame that more venture capitalists don't specialize. There seems to have been a trend over the past several years where every VC fund thought that they needed to play in every space. I think that trend is going back the other way now, somewhat. As an entrepreneur, I would much prefer to know that a venture fund specializes in a particular area of technology. Because the space is so large now that it is impossible for one organization to have adequate coverage of all the developing technologies from the Internet to semi-conductors. I would welcome the time when I could pick investors to talk with based upon their expertise rather than wasting time going to investors that might have a good track record, have large funds with successful exits but that have nothing to offer about my space.

Q: You have gone through the capital raising process several times, would you please discuss your background and talk about some of the companies that you have been involved in as an entrepreneur?

A: After I graduated from Georgia Tech in 1974, I worked in industry for a while, first at Georgia Tech Research Institute, then Scientific-Atlanta, and then at Motorola. I left my last job with Scientific-Atlanta in 1983 along with six other engineers and managers to start a company in satellite communications. I was just one of the crowd at that point, and we bootstrapped the company. We ended up selling a piece of that business to another investor which formed a spin-out company called Tridom. We got money for that through a trendy investment vehicle at the time called an R&D Limited Partnership. The IRS had very favorable tax treatments back in the 80s for companies doing research and development, and an arm of Prudential Securities ended up investing $10 million in our startup. That's how we got the company going, but again, I was one of the crowd at that point as VP of Engineering. I wasn't directly involved in the fundraising, but it was a learning experience. Our CEO also went on to get another $10 million from Federal Express. It was kind of an unusual set of investors by today's standards, but we ended up selling that company to AT&T in the late 80s, and I hung around for five years and five CEO's waiting for the supposed synergies between our little company and AT&T to develop. That never happened, and finally the 5th CEO ended that experience by firing me by voicemail when I was out of town! After that, I spent a couple of years consulting and writing business plans, which led to the formation of a company called Media4. We were located in the Georgia Tech Advanced Technology Development Center and relocated into the GCATT [Georgia Centers for Advanced Telecommunication Technology] building just before the summer Olympics in 1996. Again, that company was funded only with corporate investors. We developed the first card that you could plug into a PC that would deliver Internet over a satellite. We ended up attracting the interest of several corporate investors, but never had any VCs. That was an interesting dynamic for a small company; to have separate corporations each with their own interest investing in an early stage technology company. I have told many people, I would never do that again. We could never get them to agree on anything; one was a French company and one went bankrupt and went out of business while we were still needing seed money. Ultimately, we ended up selling the company to EchoStar, the parent company of Dish Network back in 1999. That was a unique experience from a fundraising standpoint. I left that business in 2002 and started becoming an active angel investor, which led me to the founders of JMD (Jacket Micro Devices). I helped them raise money from the local angel community, and also from VCs and came aboard as CEO.

Q: Your current company is the first time that you've raised venture money from traditional venture capital funds?

A: It really is, if you are speaking of pure venture capital. This is the first time I actually raised money myself from VCs.

Q: Having worked so closely with corporate venture in your past, describe your experience of working with the traditional VCs and how that was different?

A: With the traditional VCs, it was a longer process. The period of time where you are doing the dance and presenting your business opportunity, explaining the technology and the value proposition, just took longer than I would have expected. Because I had some relationships, we were able to bring in the angel money to kick start the process, which led to other relationships that helped bring in the venture capital.

Q: Now that you have been through the capital raising process several times, what do you now know that you wish you had known from the beginning?

A: One of the things that I learned is to very carefully pick the investors that are likely to be interested in what you were doing and really fit with you from a synergy standpoint. It's a marriage. You've got to find an investor that will understand your business and deal with the dynamics of the company. So, I would say one of the major things I've learned is to be more selective in approaching investors. That may be hard for a first-time entrepreneur who is simply trying to raise money to jump start a company. But I think it's a worthwhile exercise; really target the investors that you are going to pitch, and don't do this just by reading their website. You will have to get into the community and build personal relationships. Develop contacts you have in the industry through the attorneys, the accountants, people who know members of your board. To raise capital today, you really need that personal introduction. No one funds a business plan that is mailed in to a partner. You have to go in with a personal recommendation, a personal endorsement.

Q: After you enjoyed some initial success, you became an angel investor yourself. Did becoming an investor after being an entrepreneur change your perspective on the process?

A: Well, it makes you appreciate the other side of the table, that's for sure. I've invested in half a dozen companies as an angel, and you certainly understand the need for due diligence. I tend to ask entrepreneurs the same questions that I got asked when raising money. You can end up becoming cynical if you are not careful. If you've gone through a less than successful fund-raising campaign of your own where you've had to pitch 20 investors to find the right one, and then find the tables are turned, I found myself becoming quite cynical with the entrepreneurs. I guess I have been guilty of a kind of "what goes around comes around" attitude at times. I think it makes you a lot more careful, but I am not sure it makes you any more successful. But I am sure it certainly makes you a little more cautious as an investor because you now know what to look for and what the professional investors look for and the kind of diligence that they put companies through.

Q: How do you view the current climate for raising capital?

A: It is certainly very regionally dependent. In this part of the country – in Atlanta – I think it's doable, but difficult. Especially, outside of the angel money that's available for seed funding, capital from traditional venture sources is very difficult to get. VCs are more cautious here, they tend to invest at a later stage vs. an early stage. They tend to go with the trends in terms of hot technology; Web 2.0 and biotechnology seem to occupy

80 to 90 percent of the local investment community's time. At JMD, we are in the semiconductor industry, which is not well developed in Atlanta, so it is difficult.

Q: Do you find that entrepreneurs are looking elsewhere for capital?

A: Very much so. With the relatively few capital sources that are in Atlanta or in Georgia, it quickly becomes a regional search and then a national search for an early stage company. The good news is the out of state VCs want to come here, and they invest more heavily than local VCs do. There is a lot of activity with firms from the Northeast, the West Coast and Texas. The investment community, once you get out into the Southeast is a little better than in Atlanta, but not a lot better.

Q: Atlanta has a reputation for being a vibrant business city, why do you think the venture market is not well-developed?

A: Because it's just the wrong type of business town. Atlanta is known for enterprise information technology and media, but those are not very active, hot areas of investment right now. If we have a technology industry base, it's enterprise software and that's probably the most difficult thing to raise money for. Atlanta is not known for telecommunications or semiconductors, or even Internet firms, as are other areas of the country, so I think people view Atlanta as lacking a base of venture funded success stories. There are some examples otherwise, but companies that have been through the venture process and gone public are rare. Atlanta is viewed as a banking center and for its media activities which aren't relevant from a venture standpoint, and as a result, rightly or wrongly, it is viewed that getting executive talent into venture funded companies will also be difficult. I will take issue with that to some extent, it's doable; you just have to go out of the region to find some of your talent.

Q: If money is money, what is the downside of venture capital coming into the region from elsewhere?

A: There are notorious examples of West Coast funds putting money into Atlanta companies and then moving them to California. It has happened several times and it is something that the community should resist at all costs. I think entrepreneurs should resist. If you were entrepreneur with a fundable idea and someone offers you money if you locate on the West Coast, and you have few other ties to the community, then you are going to consider it. But I think it's bad for Atlanta, it's bad for Georgia Tech, and it's bad for the local investment community to let it happen.

Q: How could the investment climate change in Atlanta? Are there opportunities that could lead to an increase in the number of venture-backed companies?

A: Internet security seems to be hot. It seems like there will be never be an end to the spin-off effect of Internet Security Systems' success. And hat's off to them; they did a wonderful job. It seems like every month now we hear about another security related company getting funded. I think enterprise software is difficult, but there is a lot of infrastructure in Atlanta and a large part of trying to do an enterprise software play would mean leveraging that infrastructure for its best talent, but I think that is an extremely difficult thing to fund these days. I think where Atlanta has not capitalized is the resurgence of the telecom technology industry. People still think we are in the depression that followed the Internet and telecom bubble, which is not the case. The telecom companies are buying again and there is a healthy market for telecom technology.

Q: You mentioned the Internet bubble; what are the aftershocks that you are still seeing from that period?

A: Venture investors are still struggling with the whole value equation. One of the after effects of the bubble was the cessation of the market for initial public offerings, and it's not come back to even average levels by my perspective. When you look at exits, the opportunity to get reasonable multiples of invested capital through an IPO is difficult. The 10X returns that professional venture funds look for are very difficult to get in today's climate when exits are acquisitions, not IPO's.

Q: You alluded to this earlier, but you seem to think that it is more difficult for entrepreneurs without a Silicon Valley address to get funding. Would you elaborate?

A: It would absolutely be easier there. It is the sheer number of venture funds with offices in Silicon Valley. And as a result of all that money, there is an entire food chain that exists to support them: legal services and banking services. There is also much more access to entrepreneurs and executives who have been through multiple venture funded companies. The down side is it's an extremely expensive place to live, and there is a lot of competition for those dollars, but there certainly is a lot going for it in terms of technology ventures.

Q: For an entrepreneur without a Silicon Valley address, what would you suggest should be done to stand out?

A: Don't be one of the herd. If you are one of the herd in the Valley, and you've got great management team, you could probably get funded. If you are one of the herd outside of the Valley, I don't care who your management team is, it's going to be much more difficult. I would say that you have to avoid a business model that is a me-too approach. I would try to stand out from a business model standpoint. If you're an inexperienced entrepreneur that means go find somebody to bring in your team whose been through it and done it before. That's how I got involved here, helping Georgia Tech professors who never had any relevant business or early stage company experience. They had spent a year and a half trying to raise venture funding, and it wasn't going to happen until they got people like me and other members of the teams involved who had more business experience.

Q: When talking about the nuts and bolts of raising capital, there seems to be a variety of opinions about the role of a written business plan. What is your view on the need for a plan, and how have you approached it?

A: Well, the dirty little secret about JMD is that we have not written a full, honest to goodness business plan since our seed round. I think that can be a lesson. Some entrepreneurs over emphasize a lengthy business plan. I am not a fan of PowerPoint as an ultimate communications tool, but if you can't present your ideas in an attractive, clear, easy to understand dozen slides, then you are in trouble. I found that the questions that investors ask can be handled in a few pages. Whether it's a PowerPoint with a very good presenter or a short business plan of maybe 15 to 20 pages. That's all you need. When it comes to financial projections you should have one page for every year that you've been in business. So, if it's an early stage company, and you have more than one page of financial projections, you are over analyzing. The margin of error is so high that if you present more than one page, you are wasting your time and the investor's time.

Q: What have you found to be the essential information to include in a business plan?

A: A value proposition that explains what you are trying to do and why somebody would buy what you are going to do. The most important thing is why someone would buy your product or service versus someone else's product. Then you explain how protectable the technology is – for example, is it patentable – and where you are in terms of commercializing it. Then explain the total market that's available. Obviously investors want to see big numbers for the total market. Conclude by describing the team and its experience and capabilities.

Q: For a first-time entrepreneur, what is the first thing that he or she should do to prepare for the capital raising process?

A: Well, you have to ask yourself if you are ready to be an entrepreneur. Are you ready to devote the time it's going to take to do it? This means making your company the center point of your life for several years.

Q: What are some of the characteristics that you think an entrepreneur must posses when you are evaluating an investment opportunity?

A: A passionate belief that their technology is viable and the business model is valuable. They must be willing to work hard for it and willing to suffer through the set backs because there will be set backs. They must be prepared to change the course as needed. I've read that the average venture funded company goes through three strategic redirections, so expect that whatever you project as your primary product or service in all likelihood is going to be different than what you end up with because you will not know how the market is going to react until you get out there an put it in front of some customers.

Q: Do you find that people with corporate management backgrounds or technical backgrounds make better first-time entrepreneurs?

A: It is definitely the latter. There is something to be said for corporate experience and dealing with marketing and finance, but it's harder for them to make the transition. They don't necessarily have the passion about a particular technology and the problems that it can solve. That's why I think you see at least the founding entrepreneurs are technologists of some sort; they have a passion for their creation.

Q: What role should debt play in the capital raising process?

A: Any time you can get it, use it. It's cheaper than equity – always without question. Don't hock your house, but maxing out credit cards, borrowing money from friends and family, certainly. And borrow money from a bank if you can. It would absolutely be preferred over equity. It's the cheapest form of capital that you can find because you are not giving up ownership.

Q: How early in a company's development should the entrepreneur try to establish a relationship with the capital community?

A: The angel is going to want to see it as early as possible. Once you are ready to articulate the concept and understand the opportunity of the concept, I think angel investors want to see it. A lot of angels want to take an active role in their portfolio companies very early and guide the business plan. To approach a professional venture fund, you've got to have your act a little bit more together, have a readable business plan and be able to articulate the value proposition more clearly, more succinctly than you would perhaps be expected to attract an angel.

SUMMARY

The preceding interviews contain numerous pieces of advice that provide entrepreneurs with a unique window into the capital raising process. To conclude this compilation, I have distilled many of the salient points presented by our panel of experts into the following 12 items that any entrepreneur should consider as essential information when embarking on the process of raising capital.

1. Write a clear and concise executive summary of your business plan describing your product or service, identifying the management team and explaining your competition.
2. Create realistic financial projections that represent plausible scenarios and limit the information to only one page for every year your company has operated.
3. Build an advisory board of respected people from within your industry.
4. Research and understand your market so that explaining the competition and your company's prospects is second nature to you.
5. Answer questions from potential investors quickly and succinctly; it is always important to convey a command of the information necessary to running your business.
6. Recruit a quality management team that proves your credibility and convinces investors that you have the ability to attract talent.
7. Use industry contacts, including accountants and lawyers through networking to gain a warm introduction to potential sources of capital. Cold-calling and "blasting" a business plan to hundreds of investors is discouraged.
8. Be realistic about exit strategies. Initial Public Offerings are rare and stating this in a business plan as an expected outcome can brand an entrepreneur as naïve.

9. Avoid becoming too dependent on any one customer or supplier. Aside from the business risk, potential investors are looking for product validation from a broader market perspective.
10. Maintain constant vigilance over the allocation of resources. Potential investors are seeking entrepreneurs who can prove they understand the importance of expense control.
11. Always consider sources for debt financing to support the growth of your business when possible. By taking on debt rather than selling equity, entrepreneurs can likely retain a larger ownership stake in the company.
12. Conduct a self-assessment to determine if you are truly committed to the business and will do what investors expect to make it successful. Capital providers can easily detect someone who is making a half-hearted effort.

- Keith Herndon

About Innovations Publishing

Our mission is to promote, connect and educate emerging, privately owned ventures in the Southeast United States. We do this in three ways: by publishing news and information for investors, entrepreneurs and service providers, by providing educational and developmental programs and opportunities for entrepreneurs, and by providing research and consulting services based on our knowledge, experience and contacts.

Southeast Innovations

Since May of 2002, Innovations Publishing has delivered information for investors, entrepreneurs and others who follow emerging companies in the Southeast through its weekly e-newsletter Southeast Innovations. The subscriber-supported newsletter reports news on over 700 privately held companies and provides articles and research of interest to the regional venture community. Subscribers receive detailed profiles on two to three new ventures each week and updates on dozens more. The online catalog of standardized company profiles is available to subscribers for specific research, contact information or for browsing for investment opportunities. The subscription price for a year of Southeast Innovations, which includes up to 10 users, is a fraction of what it costs to attend just one venture conference.

RCB Eagles

Southeast Innovations includes a segment of more than 250 companies specially recognized as RCB Eagles. The Eagles program is operated in conjunction with the Herman J. Russell, Sr. International Center for Entrepreneurship at Georgia State University's Robinson College of Business. This program identifies and honors exceptional private companies in the Southeast. The

Eagles database features companies that have generated more than $3 million in revenue during the last twelve months and exhibited annual revenue growth in excess of 20% compounded over the past three years, and/or experienced headcount growth in excess of 25% compounded over the past three years.

For more information on Southeast Innovations and our RCB Eagles program, please visit our website:
www.innovationspublishing.com

Ben Dyer, President
bdyer@innovationspublishing.com

In addition to his role as president of Innovations Publishing, Dyer is the Managing General Partner of the Atlanta Life Venture Fund, a $25M co-investment fund targeted toward minority vendors to Fortune 1000 companies. Dyer heads the corporate finance practice at Jackson Securities which serves early-stage to mid-market companies. Jackson Securities, founded by the late Maynard H. Jackson, former Mayor of Atlanta, is now an affiliate of the Atlanta Life Financial Group. He is Chairman of Intellimedia Commerce, Inc., which was formed in January 1996 and is privately held. Intellimedia has engaged in the businesses of software development and of incubating emerging technology companies and is also a General Partner in Cordova Intellimedia Ventures. Dyer was previously Chairman and CEO of Comsell, Inc., a pioneering multimedia development firm, from its founding in 1983 until 1988, when it was acquired by Rupert Murdoch's News Corporation. Dyer was earlier a founder of Peachtree Software, Inc. and served as its president from inception in 1977 through September 1983. The company was sold to Management Science America in June 1981. After it was later sold to a venture group, Dyer returned as a director until its April 1994 acquisition by ADP. Dyer has served as president, chairman, and a director of the de novo Enterprise National Bank, and was also a founding director of Bank of Atlanta.

He is currently on the boards of privately-held FundRaisingInfo.com, Deposit Solutions, Inc., and Denarii Payments, Inc. He served four years on the board of public company TeamStaff (TSTF), concluding in January 2007. Dyer has concentrated his community activities on higher education. He has been president of the Georgia Tech Alumni Association, a director of the

Georgia Tech Foundation, and chairman of the Alumni Advisory Board for Tech's School of Industrial & Systems Engineering. He served a 30-month term as Chairman of the Georgia Tech Research Corporation. He is currently on the External Advisory Council of the Georgia Tech Research Institute. In March 2006 he received the Joseph Mayo Petit Alumni Distinguished Service Award, Georgia Tech's highest honor for its alumni. On October 19, 1998 Dyer was inducted as the 14th member of Georgia's Technology Hall of Fame. Dyer holds a Bachelor of Industrial Engineering degree with highest honor from Georgia Tech, and an MBA in finance from Georgia State University, also with highest honor.

Clifton V. (Buddy) Ray, Jr.
Executive Editor
bray@innovationspublishing.com

Prior to Innovations Publishing, Ray spent five years as the Director of E-Business for The Progeni Corporation, a computer services firm specializing in legacy system migration. Prior to Progeni, Ray served as executive vice president of Intellimedia Commerce, Inc. an Internet and e-commerce development and consulting firm. Ray served as Vice President of Peachtree Software as a founding employee of the accounting software firm. He was responsible for building one of the industries first "software factories" where just-in-time manufacturing techniques were used to produce large volumes of packaged software. He also was Vice President of Technology for Comsell, Inc. for five years, where he was responsible for software design, engineering, programming, testing and support for applications for real estate and the travel industry. While News Corp. owned Comsell, Ray was responsible for leading the development team on the first generation of Comsell's interactive multimedia PC system for travel agencies. Ray serves on the board of directors of Atlanta Interfaith Broadcasters, Inc., an advisory board for the National Park Service's WebRangers program and is a member of the Technology Association of Georgia and the MIT Enterprise Forum. Ray holds a Bachelor of Business Administration and a Masters of Business Information Systems from Georgia State University.

About The Interviewer

Keith Herndon, President
Internet Decisions, LLC
keith@internetdecisions.com

Herndon has extensive experience in media and technology with credentials in strategic planning, corporate investing and technology management. Before starting Atlanta-based Internet Decisions, a business research firm, he held several executive posts. He was Vice President of Planning and Product Development at Cox Interactive Media, a division of Cox Enterprises. In that role, he managed business development and the technology and operations teams. His efforts were instrumental in completing several strategic partnerships with companies such as Yahoo and MP3.com. He led technical due diligence efforts on many Cox investments in new media companies and served on the board of directors of Enkia Corp., a Cox investment recipient. Herndon has also been President of a business incubator, Vice President and General Manager of One Source Pro and Director of Operations at Cox Radio Interactive. In his early career, Herndon was a business reporter and editor at *The Atlanta Journal-Constitution*, establishing his skills as an interviewer and writer. Herndon holds a bachelor's degree from the University of Georgia and a master's degree from the University of Oklahoma. He also completed a Davenport Fellowship at the University of Missouri.

Production Notes

Design

The book cover was designed by Marie Matthews, who also provided pagination and technical services. Matthews is an accomplished Atlanta-based technologist, graphic designer and artist. Matthews was the first webmaster at Emory University and later served as Director of Community Publishing for Cox Interactive Media. Matthews is Vice President of Technology at Internet Decisions, LLC. She is also an award-winning artist, earning signature status in the Georgia Watercolor Society.

Transcriptions

The interviews contained in this compilation were transcribed by The Computer Secretary of Atlanta. A special acknowledgment goes to Tom Frolik, president, and transcribers Celeste King and Judy Headrick for their services.

Printing

The book was printed by BookMobile, a Minneapolis-based company that specializes in servicing the printing needs of over 300 trade houses, university presses, and independent publishers.